CLASSIC ROCK CLIMBS
NUMBER 11

WASATCH RANGE

UTAH

by Bret Ruckman
and Stuart Ruckman

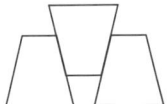

Chockstone Press
Evergreen, Colorado 80439
1997

Classic Rock Climbs: Wasatch Range, Utah

© 1997 Bret and Stuart Ruckman. All rights reserved. This book or any part thereof may not be reproduced in any form whatsoever, whether by graphic, visual, electronic, or any means other than for brief passages embodied in critical reviews and articles, without the written permission of the publisher.

Cover photo: Mindy Shulak enjoying Satan's Corner (5.8), Gate Buttress, Little Cottonwood Canyon

All photos by the authors unless otherwise credited.

ISBN: 1-57540-025-1 *Classic Rock Climbs* series
1-57540-036-7 *Wasatch Range, Utah*

Published and distributed by
Chockstone Press, Inc.
Post Office Box 1269
Conifer, CO 80433-1269

ACKNOWLEDGMENTS

Writing a guidebook involves much more than climbing routes on sunny days with friends. We have found that time on the phone is as important as time on the rock. Once again many people have gone the extra mile to get us detailed information and we owe them our sincerest thanks. Without their unmitigated help these guidebooks would never materialize. The amazing persons list: Jeff Pedersen, Lee Logston, Tony Calderone, Emery Lortsher, Drew Bedford, Brian Mecham, Douglas Heinrich, Sunni Rose, Boone Speed, Jeff Baldwin, Ron Stout, Jonny Woodward. Finally, we would like to thank our solid rock foundations–our families. The support of Kim and Fred Thalmann (and Hillary too!), Ivy Ruckman, Judy Ruckman and Libby Ellis, kept us motivated and focused. Their considerable forebearance was needed for this go-around of guidebook mayhem.

We thank you all.

TABLE OF CONTENTS

WASATCH RANGE OVERVIEW MAP iv
INTRODUCTION 1
   History 2
   Seasons and climate 2
   Crag Summary 3
   Ethics 4
   Conservation 4
   Gear and special needs 5
   Guide services and local equipment retailers 6
   Camping and amenities 6
   Emergency services 6
   Other guidebooks 7
   How to use this book 7
   Ratings 7
BIG COTTONWOOD CANYON 8
   Overview map 8
   Dogwood Crag 12
   The Dead Snag Area 12
   Storm Mountain Picnic Area 14
   Storm Mountain Island Overview Map 15
   Psychobabble Wall 18
   S-Curve Area 20
   The Pile 20
   The Millstone 25
LITTLE COTTONWOOD CANYON 28
   Overview map 28
   Little Cottonwood Bouldering 31
   Crescent Crack Buttress 33
   The Thumb 35
   The Gate Buttress Area 38
   Kermit's Wall and Perhaps Area 38
   The Green Adjective Gully 42
   The Main Gate Buttress 45
   The Dihedrals Area 48
   The Pentapitch Area 51
AMERICAN FORK CANYON 52
   Overview map 52
   Hell Area 55
   The Hell Wall 55
   Hell Cave 57
   El Diablo Wall 57
   The Cannabis Wall 60
   The Membrane 62
   The Billboard 64
   Little Mill Campground 69
   Division Wall 69
RATED ROUTE INDEX 72

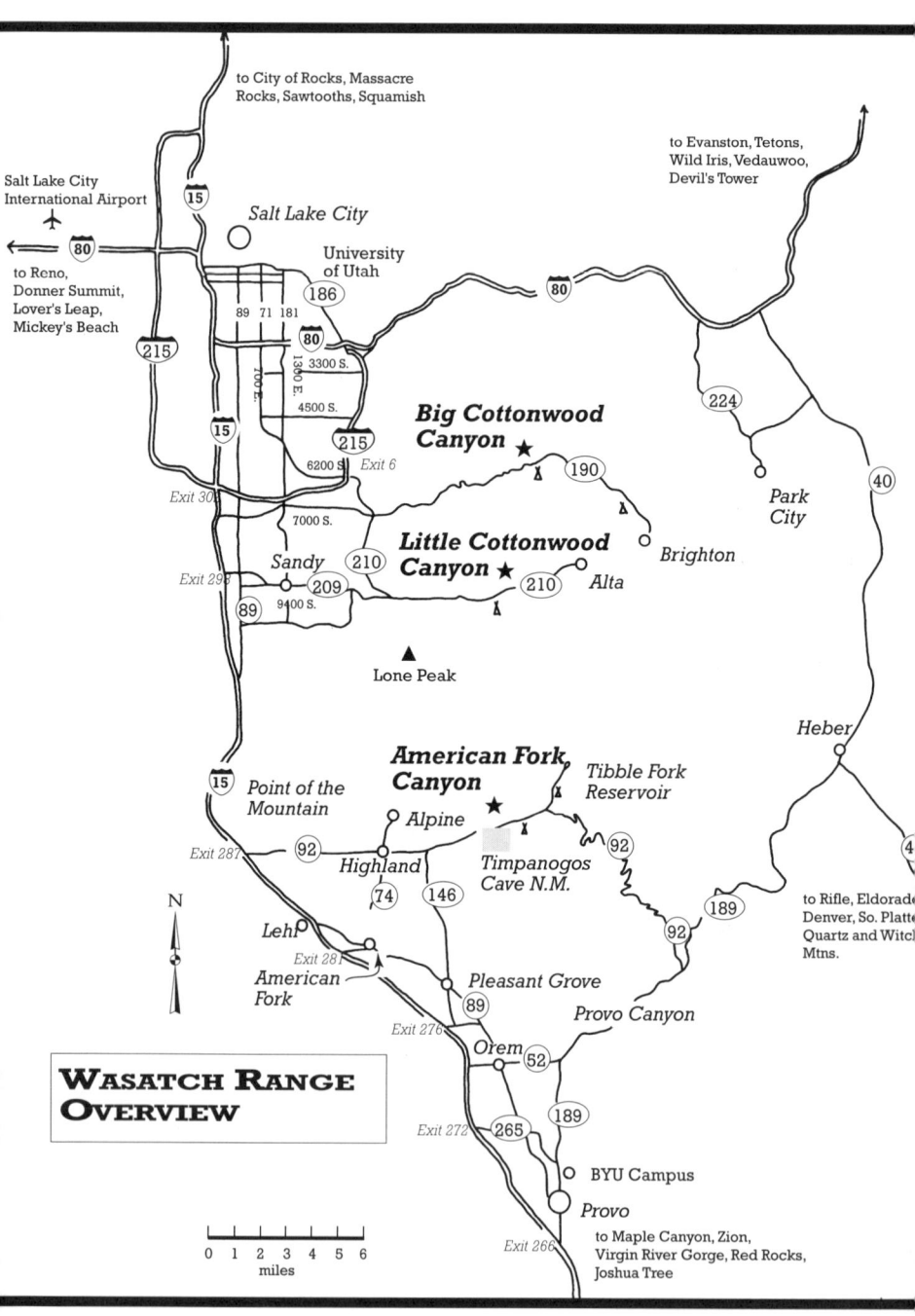

INTRODUCTION

WASATCH RANGE

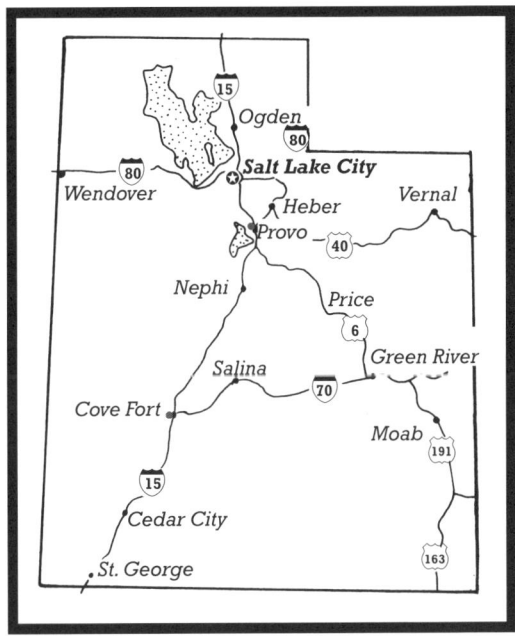

Rising dramatically above the valley floor, the Wasatch Mountains form a spectacular backdrop to the Salt Lake City/Provo metropolis. For hikers, bikers, skiers and climbers, the canyons of the Wasatch provide an intimate backyard playground, within 30 minutes of the city. This book will concentrate on three of the most popular canyons for rock climbing–Big Cottonwood Canyon (BCC), Little Cottonwood Canyon (LCC), and American Fork Canyon(AF). Each of these canyons has its own distinct flavor. Climbers will find steep, technical challenges on the quartzite faces of BCC, while the glacially-carved granite of LCC forms sweeping slabs broken by cracks and a welcome smattering of chickenheads. AF lures the sport climber with gymnastic moves on overhanging limestone. Between these three canyons the climber will find plenty of variety and loads of fun.

This book will attempt to list some of the best routes in the Wasatch Range. With a concise format like the *Chockstone Classic* series, space does not allow the inclusion of all the best routes. Therefore, our criteria for selection had several things in mind. If a cliff is extremely popular and offers a high concentration of good routes, then we included it. (Some lower quality routes have been listed simply because they are next to more classic routes.) Another factor that we tried to consider was ratings. Hopefully the range of difficulties is well-represented in this guide. The experts can tackle the test pieces in Hell while the beginner can enjoy bigger holds at Storm Mountain Island. There is some personal bias, but it shouldn't be out of hand, and we're confident you'll enjoy the excellent routes the Wasatch has to offer.

HISTORY   Please refer to our other more comprehensive guides for the history of this area.

SEASONS AND CLIMATE   Winter: When high-pressure systems settle into the Rocky Mountain region, the Salt Lake Valley is particularly prone to temperature inversions. These cold, dark, smoggy periods may be escaped neatly by climbing above the inversion layer. With solar absorption on a sunny day, several cliffs offer good climbing: in BCC, we suggest the Psychobabble Wall and in LCC the Crescent Crack area. In AF the Billboard is renowned for its winter reliability. Be prepared for snowy, mucky approaches.

Spring: Most of the rock is warm enough to climb, with the exceptions of routes at high elevations and on north-facing cliffs. Finding dry rock is another variable: Keep in mind that April is the wettest month of the year. The spring allows good climbing in the Wasatch, although the fall, as a rule, is more stable.

Summer: The creative climber can find plenty of climbing, even on the hottest days. All north-facing stuff is ready for climbers. The complex cluster of crags in BCC offer many shady nooks. LCC's south side and the bouldering at the Gate Buttress can be quite pleasant. American Fork Canyon has the swamp cooler effect at several of its crags. The long south-facing routes in LCC should be avoided.

Fall: Like most of the West, the best time of year to climb in the Wasatch is in the autumn. The temperatures are usually pleasant, so go send that project!

CRAG SUMMARY LEGEND

WASATCH RANGE • INTRODUCTION

CRAG SUMMARY

	# of routes	difficulty rating	approach time	when crag is in sun	possible to climb in rain	general angle	crack/face (majority)	sport/trad. (majority)	fingery	powerful	endurance
Big Cottonwood Canyon (quartzite)											
Dogwood Crag	2	5.11–5.13	8	part sun		slab	face	sport			endurance
The Dead Snag Area	3	5.6	10	sun		steep	crack	trad			endurance
Storm Mountain Island–East Face	6	5.5–5.10	5	sun		steep	crack	trad			endurance
Storm Mountain Island–North Face	4	5.5–5.12	5	shade		slab	face	sport		powerful	
Psychobabble Wall	8	5.10–5.12	10	part sun		steep	face	sport	fingery		endurance
The Millstone	25	5.8–5.12	30	sun		steep	face	sport		powerful	endurance
S-Curve Area	27	5.9–5.13	10	part sun		slab	face	sport			endurance
Little Cottonwood Canyon (granite)											
Crescent Crack Buttress	8	5.7–5.12	10	sun		steep		trad			endurance
The Thumb	4	5.9–5.12	25	sun		steep		trad			endurance
The Gate Buttress Area	51	5.6–5.13	15	part sun		steep		trad	fingery		endurance
The Pentapitch Area	4	5.8–5.9	20	sun		steep		trad			endurance
American Fork Canyon (limestone)											
Hell	39	5.12–5.13	5	part sun	rain	steep	face	sport	fingery	powerful	endurance
Cannabis Wall	12	5.10–5.13	5	shade		slab	face	sport			endurance
The Membrane	10	5.9–5.12	5		rain		face	sport		powerful	endurance
The Billboard	34	5.11–5.13	30	part sun	rain	steep	face	sport		powerful	endurance
Little Mill Campground Division Wall	25	5.9–5.13	5	sun		slab	face	sport			endurance

ETHICS Historically, a strong ethical ideal of establishing routes from the ground up has prevailed in the Wasatch. Many first ascents involved bold exploration of virgin rock with little assurance of success. While a route completed in this style still is the best received by the climbing community, rappel-placed bolts now are generally accepted and have shown their merits with the creation of many excellent new lines.

The Wasatch locals agree that it is absolutely taboo to add additional bolts to established routes, to cut or destroy foliage, or to create new holds (chipping, enhancement, bolting on modular holds, etc.). Please abide by these standards.

CONSERVATION In the past, climbers have been a select few, and, in general, have held a common commitment to preservation. As rock climbing has grown in popularity and now is practiced by a broader segment of the population, not all of its participants share in this commitment. The canyons surrounding Salt Lake City now are overused. This is evidenced by increased damage to trees, erosion problems, the presence of litter and human waste, disfiguring fire pits and graffiti, and unsafe water—the whole gamut of ills one associates with urban encroachment. Climbers should be leaders in the fight to save our canyons since we use—and sometimes abuse—them as much as anyone. Climbers are responsible for the ridiculously steep trails leading to the cliffs (erosional nightmares)—for overbolting, mutilating trees, strewing tape wads and Power Bar wrappers, leaving chalk, tangled masses of ugly slings on rock faces—and on and on.

What can we do? A few positive steps have been taken – like building gentler trails to the cliffs, and platforms on the steep slopes beneath popular routes. Although apparently damaging at the outset, this practice will prevent erosion over the years and will filter climbers onto one path. When scrambling up talus, climbers should remember that such slopes generally are more stable near their margins; it is less damaging to travel on the edges. Climbers should pick up their own litter, bury excrement far away from heavily-traveled areas, and minimize their impact on plant life wherever possible. The thoughtful climber also will take time to pick up litter left behind by others. Bolts and chains, when possible, should be camouflaged with colors that match the rock. When a sling is left behind, remember that earth-tone colors are preferable to neon eyesores. Chalk should be used sparingly or brushed off on popular routes and boulder problems. Climbers should remember that blaring boom boxes can ruin the outdoor experience for others.

Wasatch Range • Introduction

Let's not trash the beautiful Wasatch. The canyons are our gift to cherish, our responsibility to preserve.

GEAR AND SPECIAL NEEDS   The gear needed for a given climb is only occasionally specified in this guide. Climbers should carry RPs, nuts (at least a full set), Spring Loaded Camming Devices, quickdraws, over-the-shoulder runners, some extra carabiners and maybe some hexcentrics or tri-cams. On modern sport routes, quickdraws usually will suffice. Care must be taken here, as some routes may appear to be all bolt-protected, but in fact require some gear. In most instances, we try to mention the protection needed on these climbs. Keep in mind that old fixed pins and bolts always are suspect. In particular, be wary of pins in the quartzite, as there seems to be more shifting in quartzite than with other rock types. Bolt counts on a guidebook topo are not always accurate. Be prepared.

GUIDE SERVICES AND LOCAL EQUIPMENT RETAILERS

Black Diamond
2084 East 3900 South,
Salt Lake City
(801)278-0233

Exum Mountain Guides
(801)944-5493

Hansen Mountaineering
757 North State Street
Orem
(801)226-7498

IME
3265 East 3300 South
Salt Lake City
(801)484-8073

Mountainworks
32 South Freedom Blvd.
Provo
(801)371-0223

REI
3285 East 3300 South,
Salt Lake City
(801)486-2100

Wasatch Touring
702 East 100 South,
Salt Lake City
(801)359-9361

CLIMBING GYMS

Rock Garden
225 Freedom Blvd.
Provo
(801)375-2388

Rockreation
2074 East 3900 South
Salt Lake City
(801)278-7473

Wasatch Front Climbing Gym
427 W. Universal Circle (9160 S.)
Sandy
(801)565-3657

HOW TO GET THERE   See area finder map on page iv.

CAMPING AND AMENITIES   Ample campsites are available in Big and Little Cottonwood Canyon. There is a uniform seven-day limit, and none of the areas offer showers. However, if you are clipping bolts in American Fork Canyon, the camping can be as close as a few footsteps from the cliffs. Call 1-800-280-CAMP for campground reservations around Salt Lake City. See individual canyon introductions for more detailed information.

Because Big and Little Cottonwood Canyons are watershed for nearby Salt Lake Metropolitan area, pets are not allowed. They are allowed in American Fork Canyon.

Showers for the visiting Salt Lake area climber can be found at the following locations:
Alta Canyon Sports Center, 9565 South Highland Drive (the corner of 9400 South and Highland Drive). Showers cost $3.30 (actually the price of a swim). Their hours are M-F: 6am to 10pm, Sat. 7am to 8pm.; Sun: 12 to 5. (801) 942-2582. This is the closest place to shower for LCC.

Cottonwood Heights Recreation Center, 7500 South 2700 East. Their hours are 5am to 10pm and showers cost $4.00 (the price of a swim). (801) 943-3160. This is the closest place for BCC.

Mountain Shadow RV Park, 13275 South Minuteman Drive, Draper. (801) 571-4024. Showers cost $3.00. Roughly in between the Cottonwood Canyons and American Fork.

Campground VIP Salt Lake City, 1400 West North Temple. (801) 328-0224. Showers cost $3.00. Located near downtown–freshen up before a night on the town.

In the American Fork area:
Mountain Springs Travel Center, exit 265 on I-15 offers showers for $3.00. Their phone number is (801) 489-3622.

The Lehi Swimming Pool, 400 East 200 South, Lehi. (Take exit 281 off I-15 and drive west into the town of Lehi.) Showers cost $2.00. Open Memorial Day through Labor Day. (801) 768-7190.

Local Hotels:
The Avenues Hostel, 107 North F Street, SLC. (801) 359-3855.

The Ute Hostel, 21 East Kelsey Avenue, SLC. (801) 595-1645.

EMERGENCY SERVICES   Dial 911 from any phone for emergency service. The nearest hospitals to climbing in Big or Little Cottonwood Canyon are Alta View Hospital located at 9660 South 1300 East (801-567-2600), Cottonwood Hospital located at 5770 South 300 East (801-262-3461), and St. Mark's Hospital located at 1200 East 3900 South (801-268-7129). For

WASATCH RANGE • INTRODUCTION

American Fork, the nearest hospital is the American Fork Hospital located at 170 North and 1100 East (801-763-3300).

OTHER GUIDEBOOKS
Wasatch Climbing North and *Climber's Guide To American Fork Canyon and Rock Canyon* by Stuart and Bret Ruckman; *Climbs of the Northern Wasatch, a supplement,* by Tony Calderone.

HOW TO USE THIS BOOK The climbs in the areas described in this book are presented as topos. The form of these is pretty standard to all U.S. climbing guides. Overview maps will appear first, in detail, at the start of the chapter, and subsequently in rough with the start of major cliff descriptions.

TOPO SYMBOLS

- bolts
- ramp
- rappel
- ceiling
- crack
- overhang
- right-facing corner
- left-facing corner
- 5.10 (Highest rating on topo should correspond to the route rating in the text.)
- chockstone
- chimney
- ledge
- (2) pitch marker/belay
- route number (125a)
- bolt
- face climbing
- bush

Please send any corrections, new route information and general comments to the authors, in care of Chockstone Press, Inc., Post Office Box 3505, Evergreen, Colorado, 80437-3505.

RATINGS It is assumed the climber is aware of the current rating system (Yosemite Decimal System). On the topos, the fifth-class denotation is omitted (e.g., 5.6 becomes 6). Beware of the discrepancy in the ratings found in this book. Each area has its idiosyncrasies in regard to ratings and protection. We undoubtedly incorrectly identify the ratings of certain routes. Furthermore, we frequently have relied solely on the first ascensionist's ratings, so never take this guidebook to be definitive or infallible. Use it as a reference, as the climbing aid it is intended to be. Route lines on photos and topos are drawn to the best of our knowledge, but they, too, may not be strictly accurate.

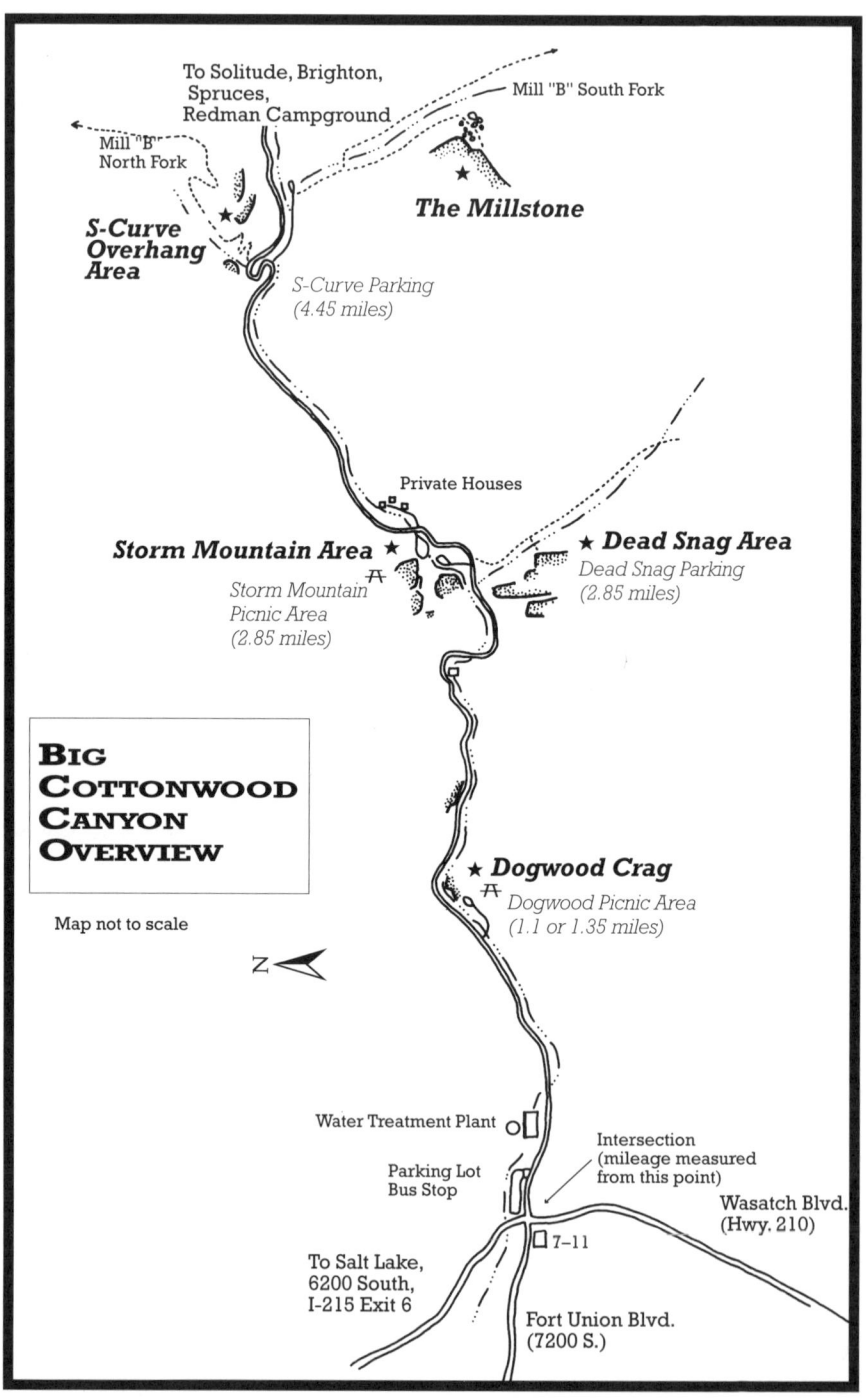

CHAPTER 1

BIG COTTONWOOD CANYON

The curving and complex Big Cottonwood Canyon (BCC) sees year-round popularity and holds an endless array of recreational opportunities. The alpine skiing is great at both Brighton and Solitude ski resorts–thus far they have avoided the "shopping mall mayhem" of many modern resorts. For the free heelers, BCC is a favorite, with loads of tours that have marvelous glade skiing, open "shots" and vistas. Climbing, hiking, mountain biking, picnicking, fishing–whatever your pleasure, you likely will find it in BCC.

At first glance, a climber might dismiss the cliffs of BCC as unworthy–they look broken, small and inconsequential. Surprisingly, the routes are fun. They offer a full spectrum of difficulties, with quality routes from 5.4 to 5.13. Once the newcomer experiences these routes, the scruffy cliffs will be seen in new light.

Mike Beck on Goodro's Wall (10c)
Photo: Jeff Baldwin

In recent years, BCC has been explored like never before. In an earlier guidebook, *Wasatch Quartzite*, the sage Harold Goodro said this about the unclimbed rock in BCC: "One has to drive up Big Cottonwood Canyon in summer, preferably in a convertible or jeep with the top down, to realize there are many climbs yet to be attempted...many have never yet been considered by the climbing fraternity." With generally short approaches, these climbs were shuffled into the category of "things to do someday." Well, someday has arrived, and energetic climbers now are scouring the canyon for new routes. The once-ignored walls suddenly have named routes–creations of the late '80s that will proliferate into the '90s.

Climbing on quartzite takes some getting used to. Beginning climbers like the quartzite because of the abundant holds, and hone-masters can climb the overhangs for the same reason. Many of the routes belie their appearance–they are steeper than you think. But the protection can be funky. Quartzite rarely allows a good pin, and hand-drilling bolts can be laborious–bordering on ludicrous–because of the hardness of the rock. Therefore, many routes require expertise with nutcraft. Bold routes characterized the harder grades until power drills entered the scene. Some of the more recent lines are completely protected by bolts, or by bolts interspersed with natural gear.

Unfortunately, history has been lost on several BCC routes, either from non-documentation or from careless bolting of purportedly "virgin" rock. Still, power drills enable bolt protection where it was practically impossible before, and constructive, thoughtful use has resulted in exciting and worthwhile routes.

BCC offers more shady crags and fewer climbers than Little Cottonwood Canyon, making it a good choice for summer. Several crags bode well for winter climbing as well, resting high on the south faces of the canyon. Especially popular among the novice climbers is the Storm Mountain picnic area, where a picnic can follow an afternoon of pleasant climbing.

The routes will be listed in the order they are reached when driving up the canyon.

CAMPING In Big Cottonwood Canyon, check out Spruces Campground, located 9.8 miles up the canyon. It offers 121 campsites (97 non-reservation) at $11 per night. Also in Big Cottonwood Canyon is Redman Campground, located 13.2 miles up canyon a half-mile past the last entrance to Solitude ski resort. Redman offers 50 sites at $11 per night.

AMENITIES At the mouth of BCC is the intersection of Wasatch Blvd. and Fort Union Blvd. A 7-11 store on the southwest corner of this intersection sells gas and has an automatic teller machine (ATM). Driving south on Wasatch Blvd. from this intersection will bring you to the next stoplight, at the corner of Wasatch Blvd. and 7800 South. Turn right here and one block west there is a Smith's grocery store and an ATM.

Big Cottonwood Canyon

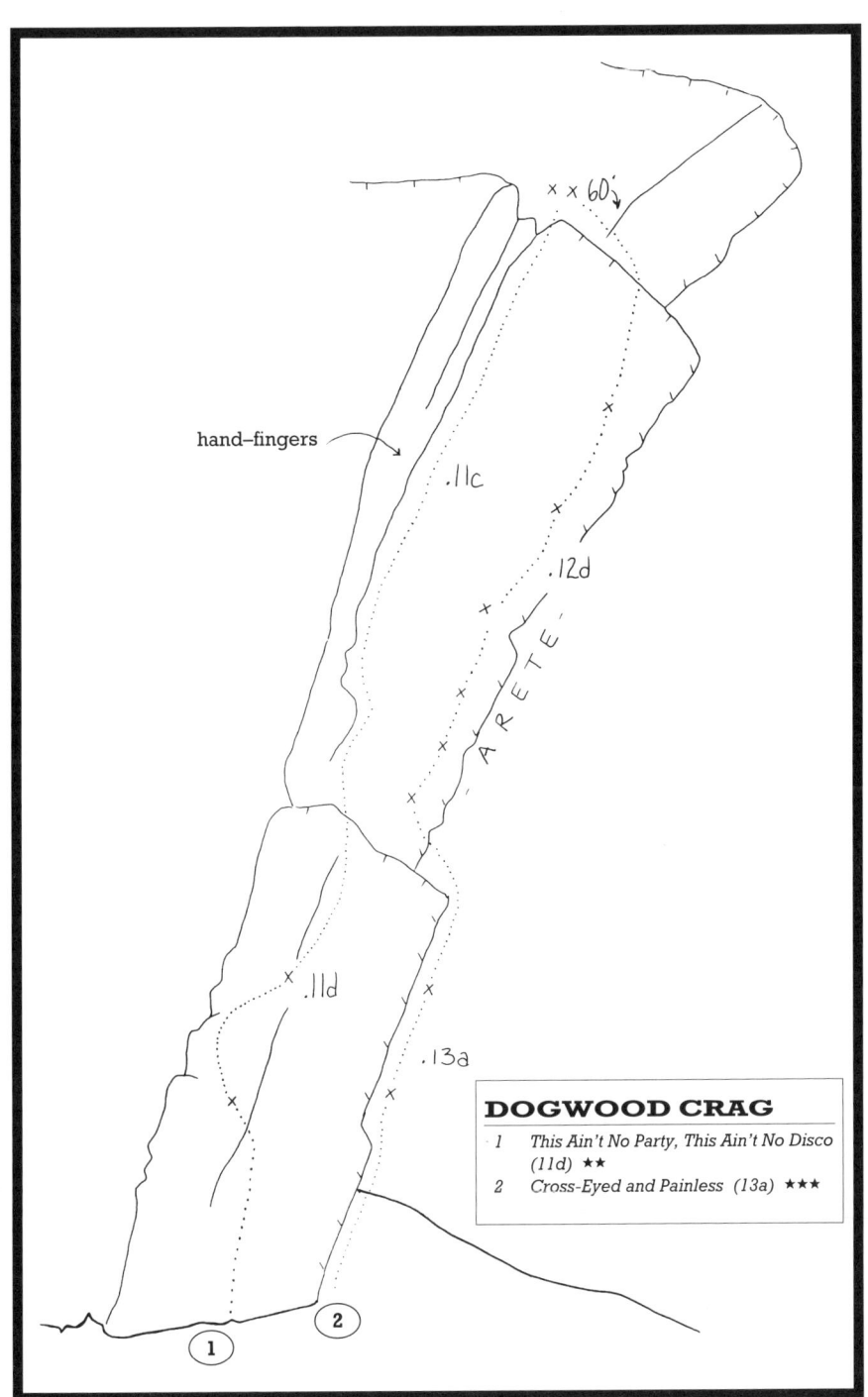

DOGWOOD CRAG

Just beyond the Dogwood Picnic area on the south side of the road is the Dogwood Crag. The routes rise out of (or nearly out of) the Big Cottonwood Stream, and are characterized by water polished holds. The two climbs listed here are on the far east side of the crag. They are overhung and shady in the mornings.

APPROACH   *1.1 miles up canyon from the intersection at the mouth of the canyon is the Dogwood Picnic Area. This is a U.S. Forest Service fee area, so either park on the road and walk in ($2.00), or drive in and park ($4.00 per vehicle). From the furthest east parking area in the picnic ground, walk up a trail that takes you to the top of the crag. Keep walking east and you'll eventually be able to switchback down to the base of the routes. During lower water times, simply park up canyon a bit farther on the main road and jump rocks across the stream. See canyon overview map on page 8.*

DESCENT   *Lower off chains at the top of the formation.*

   1 **This Ain't No Party, This Ain't No Disco (11d)** ★★   Bring a #2 Friend, among other hand and finger-sized gear.

   2 **Cross-Eyed and Painless (13a)** ★★★   Classic arête.

THE DEAD SNAG AREA

This large, east-facing wall rests at a kind angle and offers many fine routes on excellent quartzite. A short approach, longer routes, and moderate grades have made this area popular. The lines follow clean crack systems, however, face climbing predominates, due to the square holds that abound.

APPROACH   *Park 2.85 miles up canyon from the intersection at the mouth of the canyon. This is directly across from the entrance to the Storm Mountain Picnic Area. Eighty feet up canyon from the Storm Mountain sign, a dirt road heads right (southwest) towards a talus slope. Walk up this road, skirting underneath the talus, past some water pipes, for a short quarter mile. The trail levels off and immediately the surrounding brush opens up to a good view of the Dead Snag Area. Stop here. A trail cuts off right (west), descending through the brush to the stream. Cross the creek at the easiest point, then walk up stream roughly thirty feet to catch the trail on the other bank. This meanders through the trees to reach the base of the wall. The start of Steort's Ridge is not so obvious. It begins a few feet left (south) of a prominent arête that forms the edge of a large, broken right-facing corner. Please see canyon overview, page 8.*

DESCENT   *Three one-rope rappels are possible from the top of the East Dihedrals. An alternate descent involves some scrambling, but only one short rappel. From the top of the routes, walk south along the prominent ledge*

Big Cottonwood Canyon • The Dead Snag Area

THE DEAD SNAG AREA

3 East Dihedrals (6) ★★
4 Jig's Up (6) ★★
5 Steort's Ridge (6) ★★★

system. Scramble down and around the corner as the ledge narrows to a pine tree. A sixty foot rappel reaches the ground. See photo, page 13.

   3   **East Dihedrals** (6) ★★   Good climbing in right-facing dihedrals.
   4   **Jig's Up** (6) ★★   Thin crack climbing on good rock.
   5   **Steort's Ridge** (6) ★★★   Exciting arête climbing.

STORM MOUNTAIN PICNIC AREA

APPROACH   Park 2.85 miles up canyon from the intersection at the mouth of the canyon. The Storm Mountain picnic area is a U.S. Forest service fee area, and you can park inside the picnic area for four dollars per car, or park on the main highway and walk in for two dollars per person. All the approaches are quite straightforward and are described in detail at the beginning of each wall. See overview map, pages 8, 15.

STORM MOUNTAIN ISLAND–EAST FACE

The "island" is a blob of quartzite bounded by a large field on the north, the Storm Mountain Picnic Area on the east, and the Big Cottonwood Creek and highway on the south. It has been a principal climbing area in Big Cottonwood Canyon from the beginning, and offers a good selection of moderate to extreme routes on good rock. During spring high-water periods some of the climbs on the south end are hard to access.

APPROACH   Walk or drive to the parking area near the spillway of the dam, and cross the river on the bridge. For routes 6 through 9, turn left just after the bridge and follow the paved path past two picnic tables near the river. Continue along the edge of the water until a ledge system is reached that allows a southward traverse to the base of the routes. For the Goodro's wall area, routes 10 and 11, turn left after the bridge, then take the right fork until the trail passes several small boulders between two picnic tables. Turn left (south) and march up the talus to an easy third class corner which accesses the routes. See Storm Mountain Overview, page 15.

DESCENT   Except for Goodro's Wall and Six Appeal, all routes reach the top of the "island." To descend, walk off west, then follow one of the paths that heads down to the north. The main trail can be picked up here, near the power line, and followed back to the bridge across the stream. For Goodro's and Six Appeal, simply lower or rappel off the chains at the top of each route.

   6   **Nice Little Crack** (5) ★
   7   **Storm Mountain Stupor** (5) ★
   8   **Le Creme de Shorts** (9) ★★
   9   **Layback Crack** (5) ★★

Big Cottonwood Canyon • Storm Mountain Overview 15

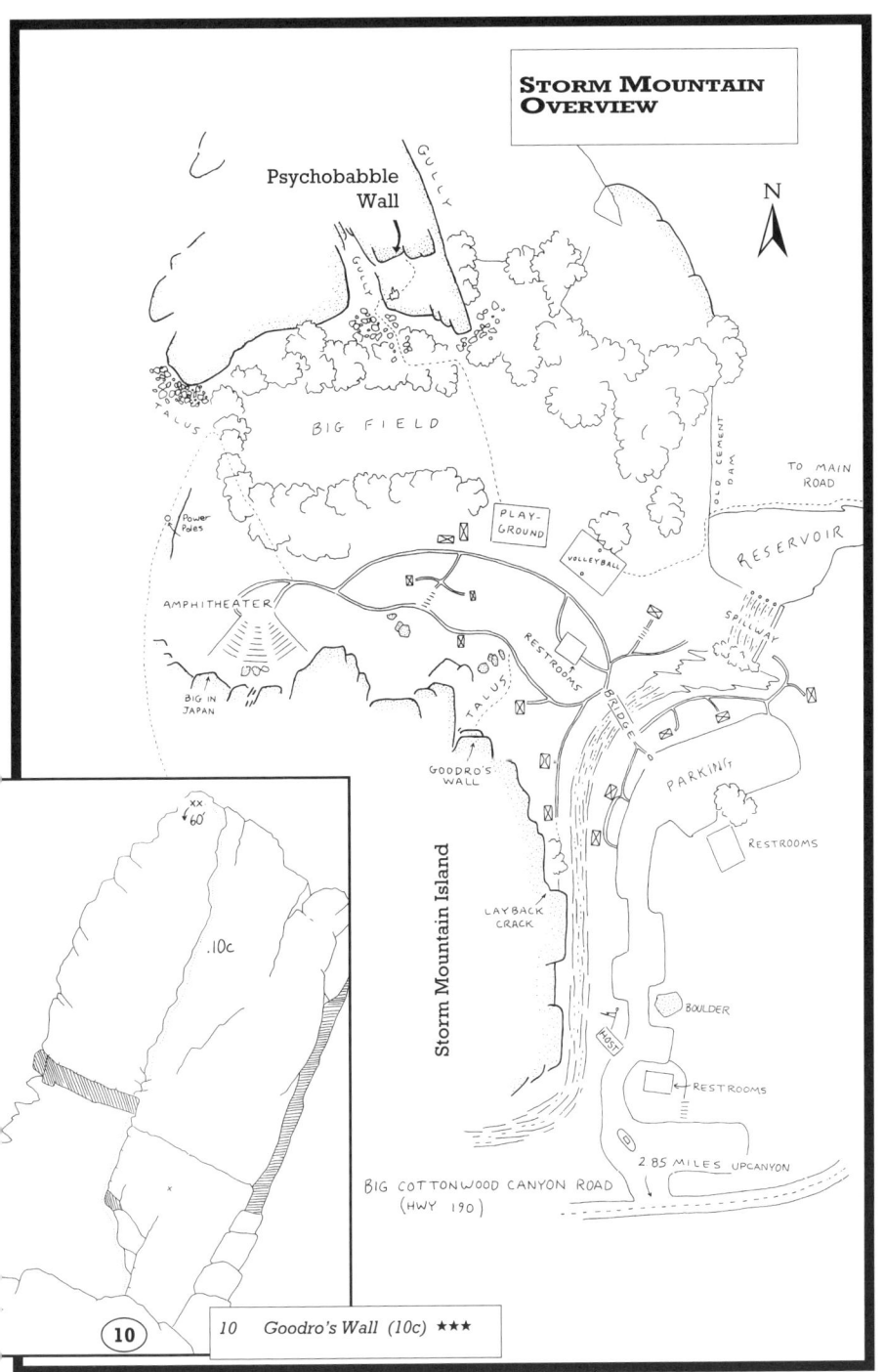

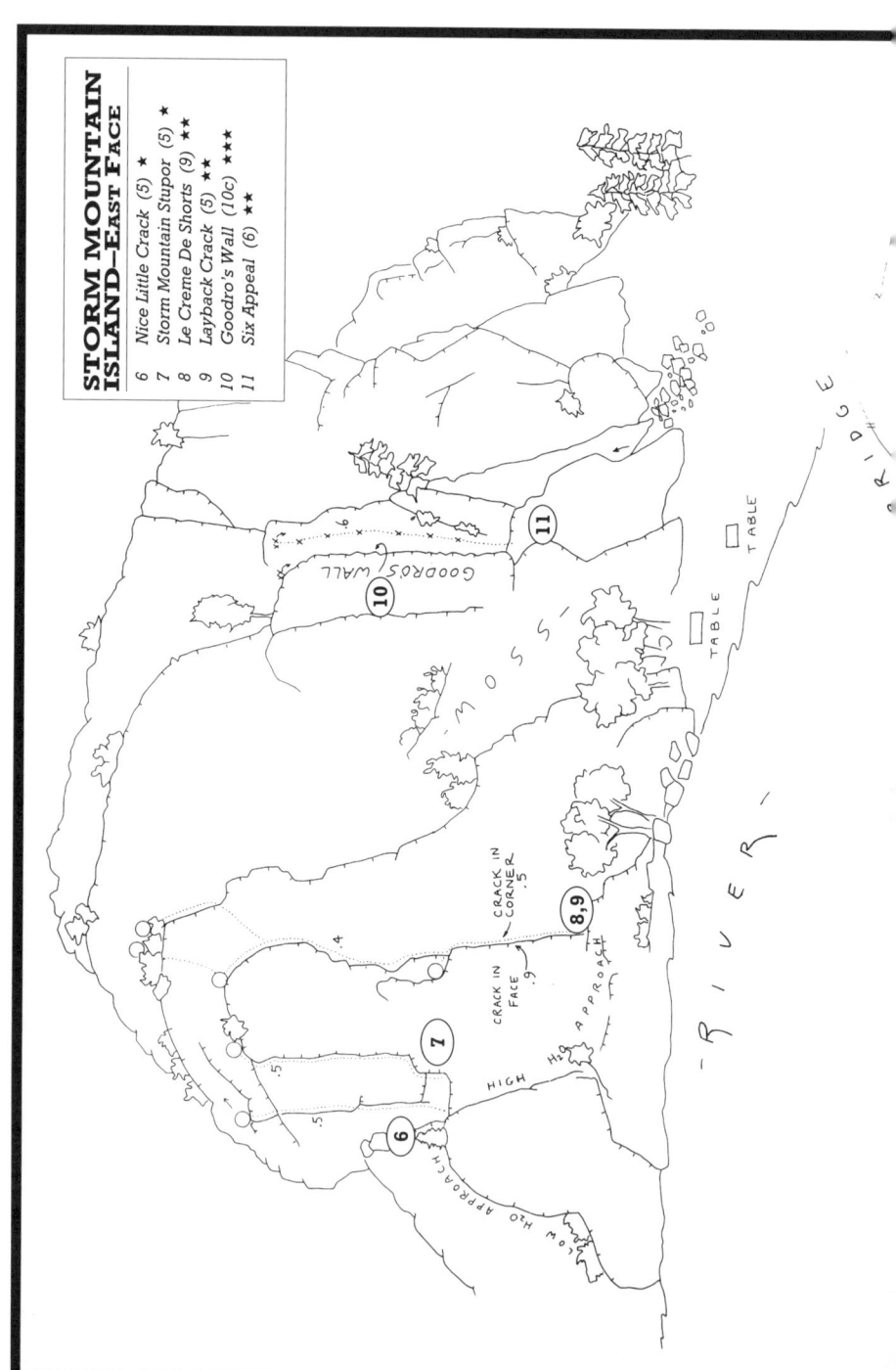

Big Cottonwood Canyon • Storm Mountain Island

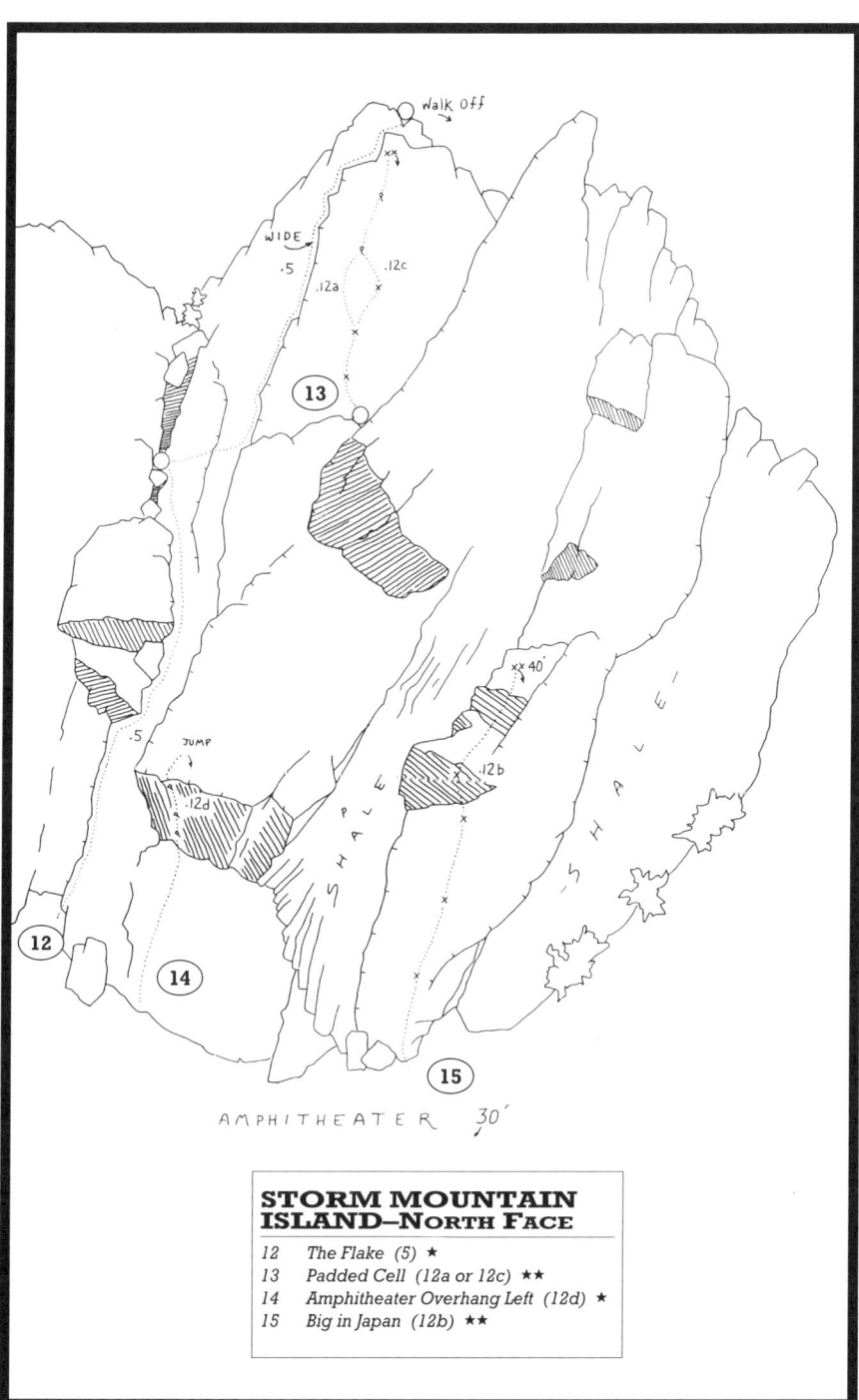

STORM MOUNTAIN ISLAND—North Face

12   The Flake (5) ★
13   Padded Cell (12a or 12c) ★★
14   Amphitheater Overhang Left (12d) ★
15   Big in Japan (12b) ★★

10 Goodro's Wall (10c) ★★★   Bring gear to 2 inches. Overhung crack climbing.
11 Six Appeal (6) ★★   One of the easiest sport routes in the Wasatch.

STORM MOUNTAIN ISLAND–NORTH FACE

Shady, even in summer. These routes sit just above the amphitheater.

APPROACH   See the approach for the East Face. Continue walking past the cut off for Goodro's Wall, until the amphitheater is reached. Walk up the stairs to the base of the routes. See Storm Mountain Overview, page 15.

DESCENT   Lower off chains for all of these routes, except for Amphitheater Overhang Left, where you just jump off after the hard bit, and The Flake where a walk off west meets the main trail near the power line, and a switchback below the power line brings you back to your packs.

12 The Flake (5) ★
13 Padded Cell (12a or 12c) ★★
14 Amphitheater Overhang Left (12d) ★   A huge dyno needs to be executed.
15 Big in Japan (12b) ★★   Brief, but good grief!

PSYCHOBABBLE WALL

From a distance this wall appears insignificant and broken. At the base of the routes, however, the wall has a different character: overhanging and solid. Overhanging arête climbing, pumper crack moves and thin face problems are all found on this wall. It faces south and therefore can be a good choice on chilly days with sun. Bring an assortment of gear up to this wall, with emphasis on small nuts and RPs.

APPROACH   From the playground area, walk north across the field to an open area in the trees with a steep trail. Walk up this trail for twenty feet, turn left (west) and walk along another trail for fifty feet, then turn right (north) and walk up talus to the gully west of the Psychobabble Wall. Walk up this gully a bit, to a break in the cliff by a box elder tree. From here some moderate scrambling leads to the base. See Storm Mountain Overview, page 15.

DESCENT   These routes have anchors at the top and can be descended with one rope, or do an easy down climb to the east.

16 The Enemy Within (12a) ★★★   Thrilling arête climbing.
17 The Eye of the Enemy variation (11b) ★★
18 Eye In The Sky (12a/b) ★★★   Bring those RPs. A bold test piece.
19 Psychobabble (10b/c) ★★★   Varied and excellent.

BIG COTTONWOOD CANYON • PSYCHOBABBLE WALL

PSYCHOBABBLE WALL

16 The Enemy Within (12a) ★★★
17 The Eye of the Enemy variation (11b) ★★
18 Eye In The Sky (12a/b) ★★★
19 Psychobabble (10b/c) ★★★
20 Psychostematic (10a) ★★
21 Rebel Yell (11c) ★★
22 Rock Capades (10d) ★★
23 Eyes Without a Face (11a) ★★

20 Psychostematic (10a) ★★
21 Rebel Yell (11c) ★★   Bring a number two Friend and some medium nuts.
22 Rock Capades (10d) ★★   RP type nuts recommended.
23 Eyes Without a Face (11a) ★★   RP type nuts recommended.

S-CURVE AREA

Bolt protected climbing has made the S-Curve Area into a vastly popular climbing locale, with plenty to choose from in a variety of grades. Overhangs pervade this area, and most of the routes tackle them in some capacity. Even the huge overhang at the left end of the wall now sports three routes. Most of these routes are south-facing.

APPROACH   Park 4.45 miles up canyon from the intersection at the mouth of the canyon. There is a small parking lot between the turns of the big "s" curve in the road, and additional parking on the right side of the first curve. Stairs lead from the parking area to the road at the top of the "s"curve. Cross the highway. For the routes at The Pile, routes number 24 through 28, continue straight ahead on a path that follows the small creek. After one hundred feet the climbs will be obvious on the left (west) side of the creek. To reach the S-Curve Area follow the hiking trail right (east). At the end of the third switchback continue straight ahead on a climber's trail to reach the base of the wall. See canyon overview page 8.

DESCENT   Except for two routes, the Alpenbock Route and Tres Facile, all routes can be descended using one rope. Several routes require two rappels. See topo, page 22-23.

THE PILE

The Pile is unbelievably popular, due to its twenty second approach, cool temperatures and bolt-protected overhanging climbing.

24 Gomer Pile (10a) ★
25 Left Pile (12b) ★★   Ruthlessly difficult.
26 Pile Surgery (12a) ★   Misses both cruxes, but still has good climbing.
27 Right Pile (11d) ★★   The clock is ticking–pump it out.
28 Dog Pile (10b) ★

S-CURVE AREA

29 Dog Eat Dog (13d) ★★★   Big pulls off bad slopers. Jump off at the ramp on the *S-Curve Overhang* route.
30 S-Curve Overhang (11c) ★★   Bring long runners.

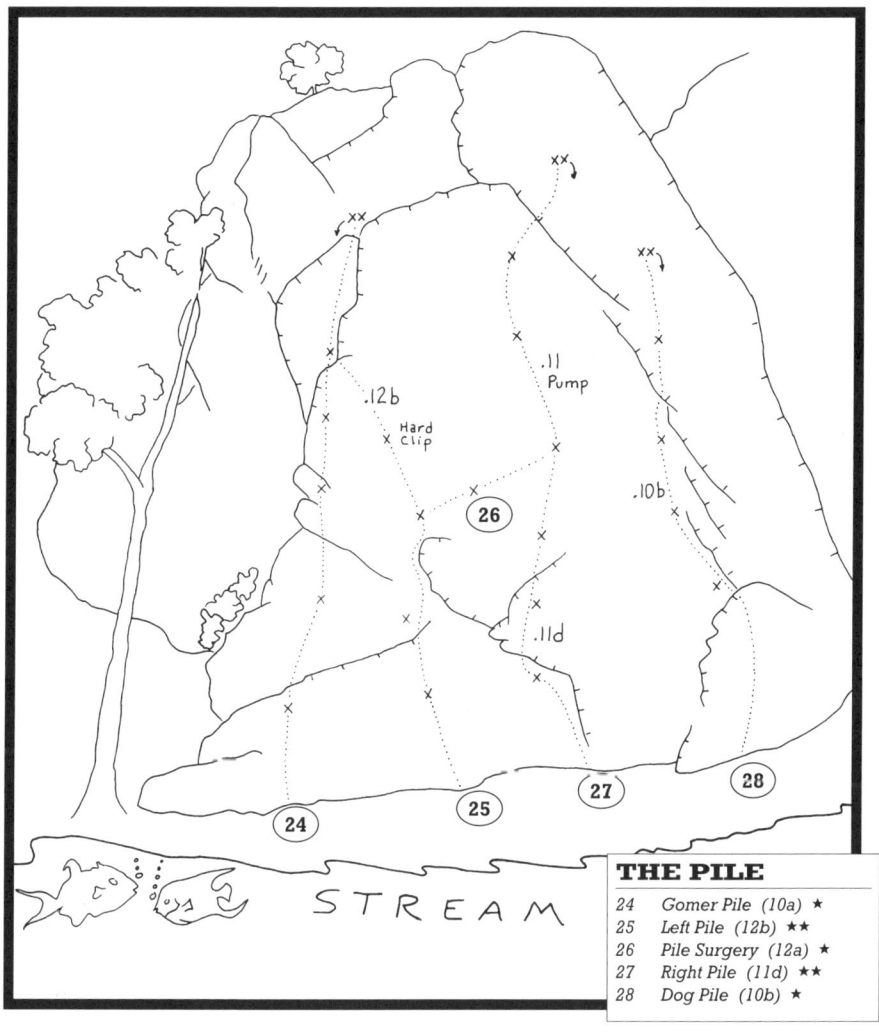

THE PILE

24	Gomer Pile (10a)	★
25	Left Pile (12b)	★★
26	Pile Surgery (12a)	★
27	Right Pile (11d)	★★
28	Dog Pile (10b)	★

31 **High Life (12c)** ★★★ Exposed and pumpy.
32 **Old Route (8)**
33 **Melting Point (10b)** ★ Strenuous and harder if you're shorter.
34 **Clastic Cling (10d)** ★ Use long runners.
35 **Ionic Bonding (11a)** ★★ Exposed and tricky second pitch moves.
36 **Alpenbock Route (9)** ★ Look for old pins and bring gear.
37 **Mass Wasting (11c)** ★★ Bring a few long runners and big guns.
38 **Red Light District (9+)** ★ Deceptively difficult.

S-CURVE AREA • BIG COTTONWOOD CANYON

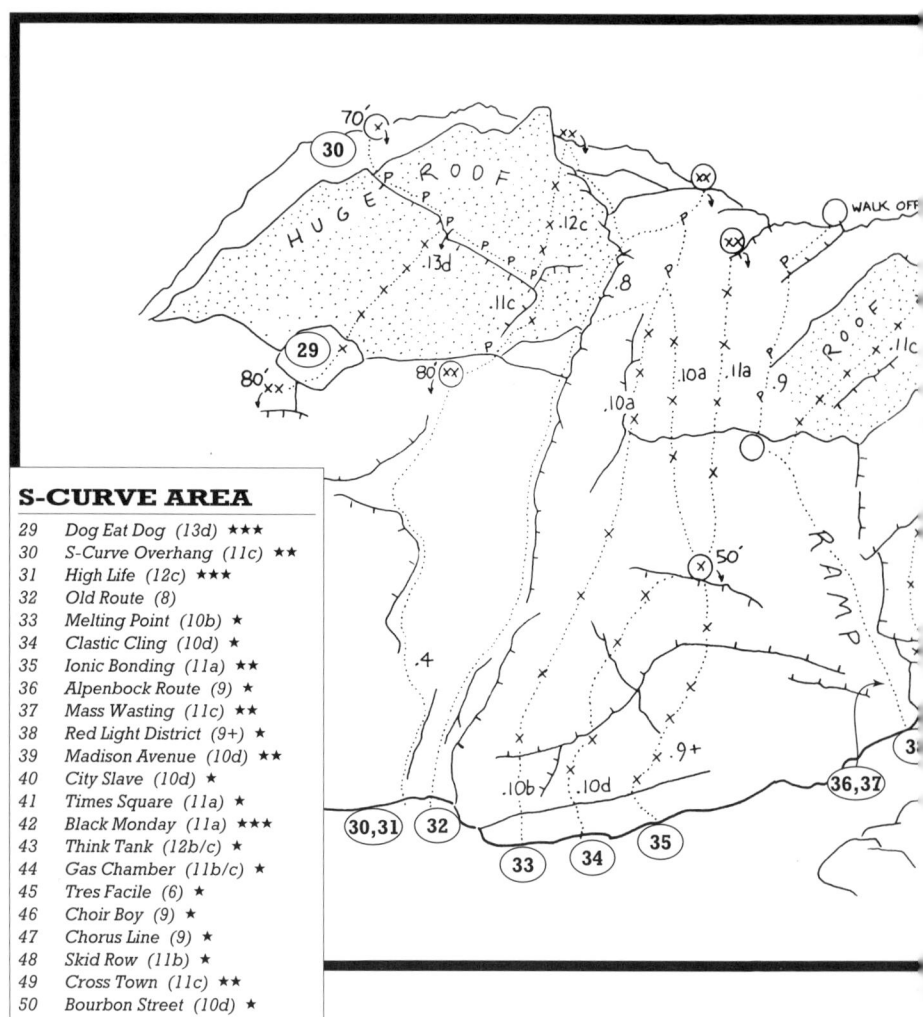

S-CURVE AREA

#	Route	Stars
29	Dog Eat Dog (13d)	★★★
30	S-Curve Overhang (11c)	★★
31	High Life (12c)	★★★
32	Old Route (8)	
33	Melting Point (10b)	★
34	Clastic Cling (10d)	★
35	Ionic Bonding (11a)	★★
36	Alpenbock Route (9)	★
37	Mass Wasting (11c)	★★
38	Red Light District (9+)	★
39	Madison Avenue (10d)	★★
40	City Slave (10d)	★
41	Times Square (11a)	★
42	Black Monday (11a)	★★★
43	Think Tank (12b/c)	★
44	Gas Chamber (11b/c)	★
45	Tres Facile (6)	★
46	Choir Boy (9)	★
47	Chorus Line (9)	★
48	Skid Row (11b)	★
49	Cross Town (11c)	★★
50	Bourbon Street (10d)	★

39 **Madison Avenue (10d)** ★★ Again, deceptively steep.

40 **City Slave (10d)** ★ A roof problem.

41 **Times Square (11a)** ★ Tricky lip sequence.

42 **Black Monday (11a)** ★★★ Ever popular.

43 **Think Tank (12b/c)** ★ A necessary dyno leaves many mystified.

44 **Gas Chamber (11b/c)** ★ The right route on the upper roof.

45 **Tres Facile (6)** ★

Big Cottonwood Canyon • S-Curve Area

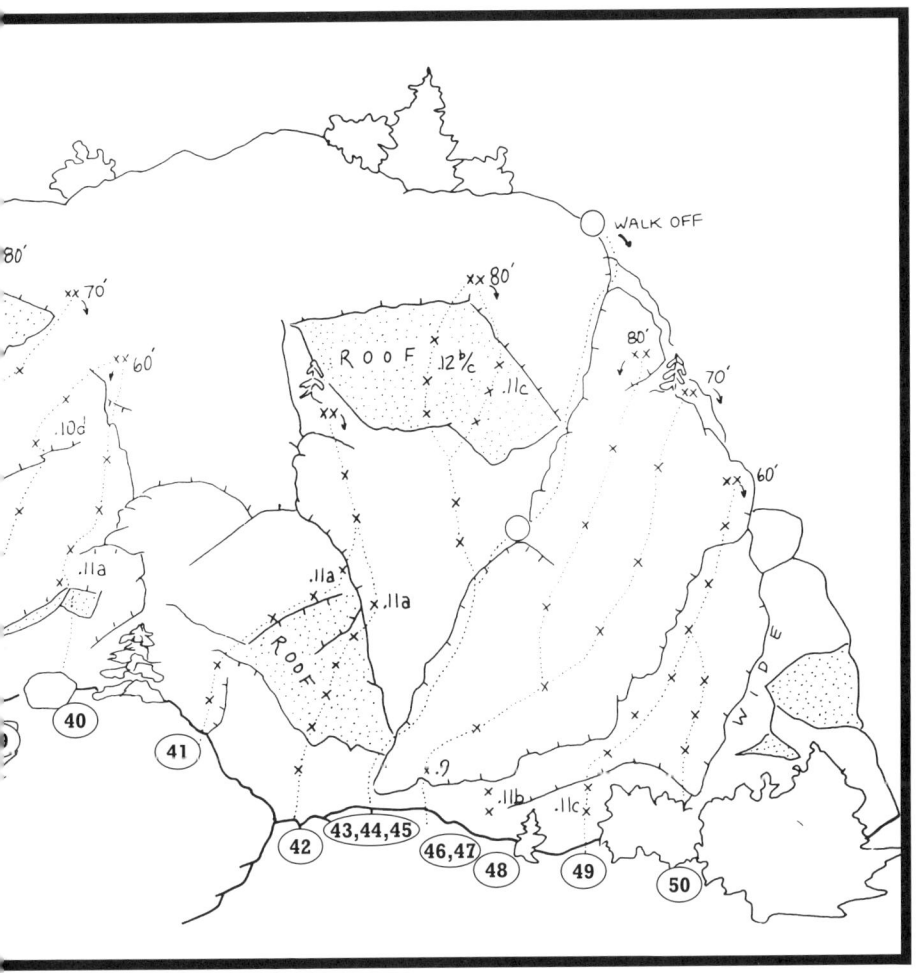

46 **Choir Boy (9)** ★ Climbs up the center face after *Chorus Lines'* third bolt.
47 **Chorus Line (9)** ★ Crank the roof, then cruise.
48 **Skid Row (11b)** ★ Long reaches at the crux.
49 **Cross Town (11c)** ★★ Hard and devious climbing. Big jug finish.
50 **Bourbon Street (10d)** ★ A direct start to *Cross Town*.

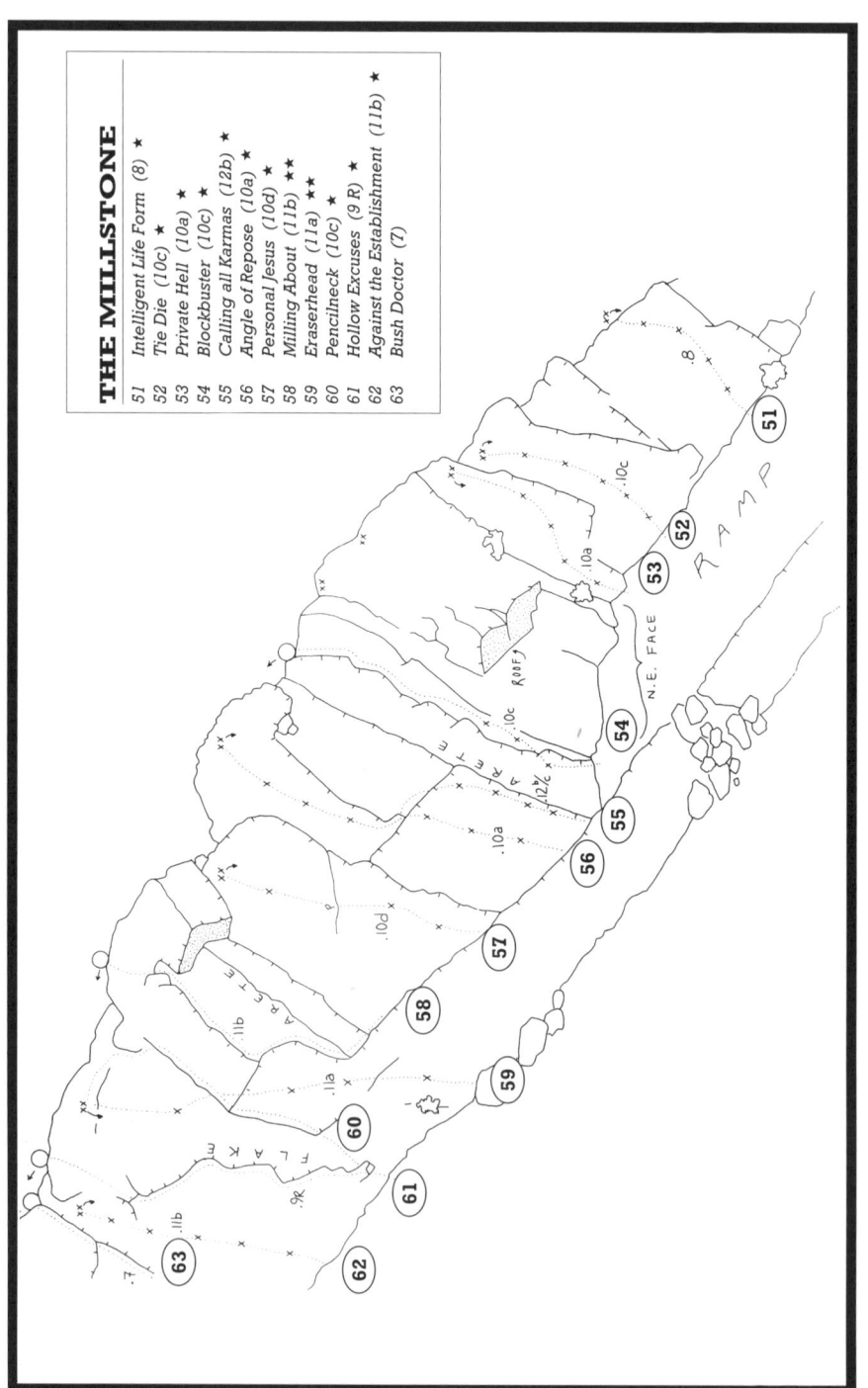

THE MILLSTONE

The first huge slab on the west side of the Lake Blanche Trail has a broad, vertical, southeast face. This face offers a high concentration of quality vertical to overhanging routes that are mostly bolt protected. Expect sun in the mornings, shade in the afternoons and dramatic views of the upper cirque from atop the climbs.

APPROACH *4.4 miles up canyon from the intersection at the mouth of the canyon, a small spur road comes in from the right and leads to a parking lot at the trailheads for the Broad's Fork and the Lake Blanche Trail. Park here and walk up the spur road toward the Lake Blanche Trail. The trail begins three hundred feet down canyon from the end of the road, right where the road crosses the creek. The main hiking trail follows the west side of the creek for a quarter mile to a bridge. The climbers trail to the Millstone doesn't cross the bridge, instead it stays on the right (west) side of the creek. Follow this path as it parallels the stream, climbs a short, steep bank, then continues paralleling the stream from the slopes above. Eventually this trail levels out and ends in a thicket. Twenty feet before this impasse, a drainage enters the trail from the right (west). Walk up this stream bed for forty feet, step left and follow the trail south again to the base of some massive talus. The Millstone is the steep wall that forms the right flank of the talus. Walk straight up the talus, traversing rightward just below The Millstone to reach the base of the wall. Expect this to take around 35 minutes. See canyon overview page 8.*

DESCENT *All routes can be descended with one rope. Several routes, however, require a belay at the top of the cliff, and then an upward shuffle on the slab to reach the tree at the top of Miller Time for a rappel off. See topos, pages 24 and 26.*

The routes are described from right to left on the cliff.

- 51 **Intelligent Life Form** (8) ★
- 52 **Tie Die** (10c) ★
- 53 **Private Hell** (10a) ★
- 54 **Blockbuster** (10c) ★   Climb the severely overhung northeast face.
- 55 **Calling all Karmas** (12b) ★   A difficult, balancey start to *Angle of Repose*.
- 56 **Angle of Repose** (10a) ★
- 57 **Personal Jesus** (10d) ★
- 58 **Milling About** (11b) ★★   Bring #$1\frac{1}{2}$ Friends for this corner.
- 59 **Eraserhead** (11a) ★★   Bring a few small pieces for the crack.
- 60 **Pencilneck** (10c) ★   Bring small gear.

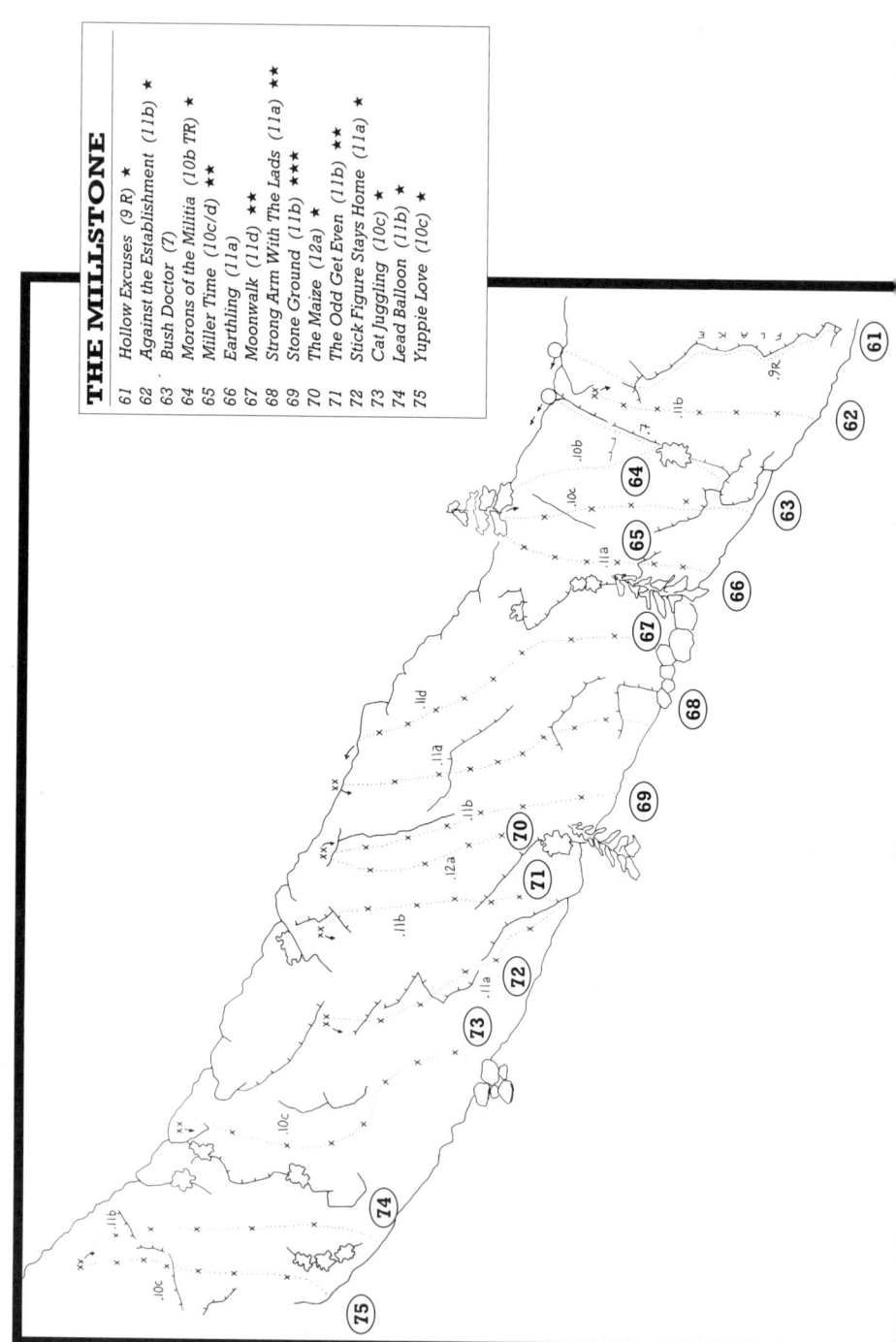

THE MILLSTONE

61 Hollow Excuses (9 R) ★
62 Against the Establishment (11b) ★
63 Bush Doctor (7)
64 Morons of the Militia (10b TR) ★
65 Miller Time (10c/d) ★★
66 Earthling (11a)
67 Moonwalk (11d) ★★
68 Strong Arm With The Lads (11a) ★★
69 Stone Ground (11b) ★★★
70 The Maize (12a) ★
71 The Odd Get Even (11b) ★★
72 Stick Figure Stays Home (11a) ★
73 Cat Juggling (10c) ★
74 Lead Balloon (11b) ★
75 Yuppie Love (10c) ★

Big Cottonwood Canyon • The Millstone

61 Hollow Excuses (9 R) ★ Scary moves and protection.
62 Against the Establishment (11b) ★
63 Bush Doctor (7)
64 Morons of the Militia (10b TR) ★ Climb the face right of *Miller Time*.
65 Miller Time (10c/d) ★★ Technical crux.
66 Earthling (11a)
67 Moonwalk (11d) ★★
68 Strong Arm With The Lads (11a) ★★ Overhangs galore.
69 Stone Ground (11b) ★★★ Reachy and pumpy.
70 The Maize (12a) ★ Thin.
71 The Odd Get Even (11b) ★★ Remember those feet.
72 Stick Figure Stays Home (11a) ★ Some flexi-flakes grace the top.
73 Cat Juggling (10c) ★ One of the longest at the Millstone.
74 Lead Balloon (11b) ★ Increasingly hard to a wicked crux.
75 Yuppie Love (10c) ★

Paul Hodges on *Madison Avenue* (10d)
Photo: Jeff Baldwin

28 • LITTLE COTTONWOOD CANYON

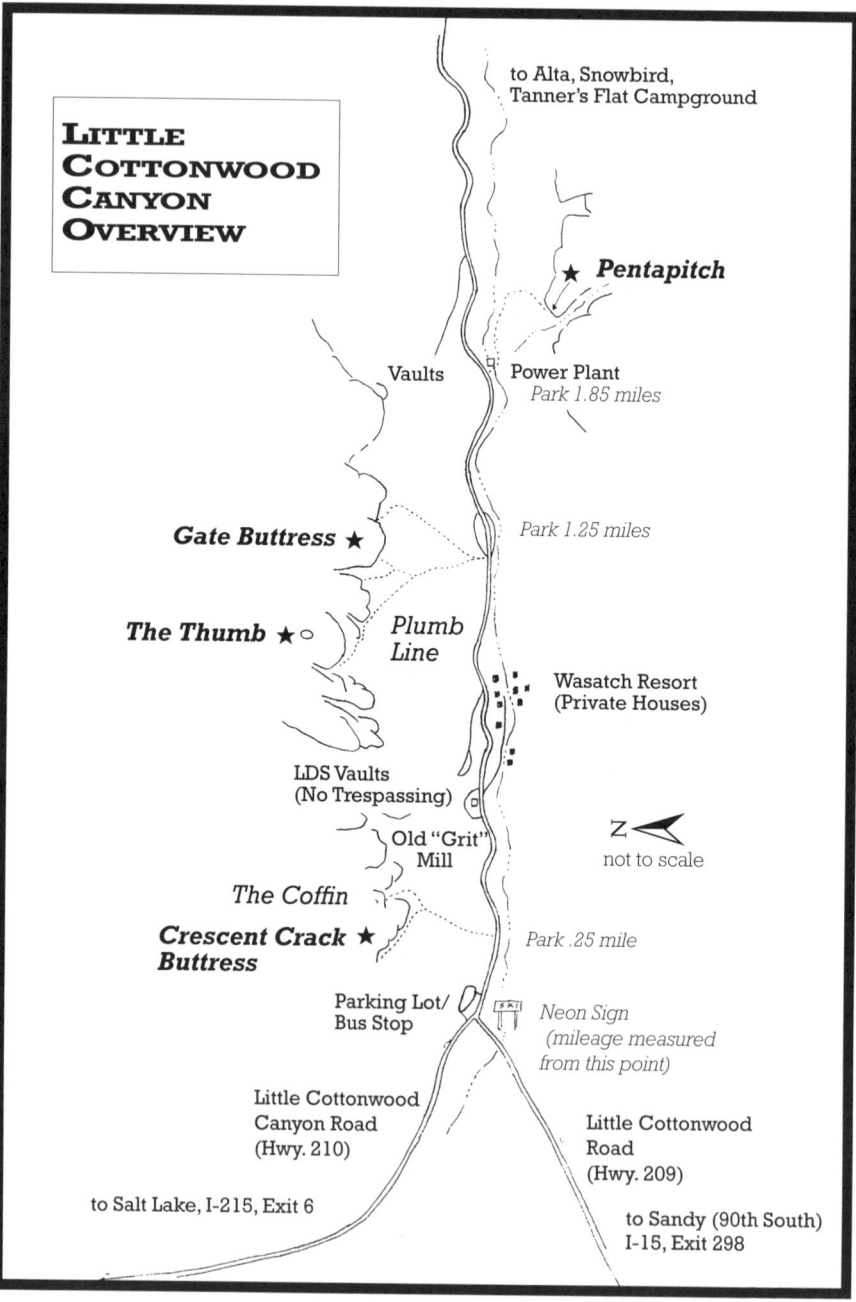

CHAPTER 2

LITTLE COTTONWOOD CANYON

Little Cottonwood Canyon (LCC) is a recreational haven. The U-shaped, glacially-carved valley is visited by hundreds of thousands of people each year—a small percentage of whom are climbers. Snowbird and Alta, bustling at the head of the canyon, maintain reputations as world-class ski resorts, and what the locals say is true: the snow dumps here. Usually it's the light, low-density stuff that provides fantastic backcountry skiing as well. In summer, the canyon offers pleasant temperatures, scenic hikes (wildflowers galore in July and August), peak-bagging amongst bountiful 11,000-foot summits, festivals, concerts, tram rides—and, of course, rock climbing.

Brian Mecham climbing on the Gate Boulders.

The rock climbing, for the most part, is on granite. The vast majority of the routes are on the north side, and in the lower third of the canyon. A potpourri of climbing styles come into play here, but the rock lends itself predominantly to face climbing. Rock quality on the more popular routes is excellent, although flaky rock may be encountered on certain of the more obscure climbs.

In winter, the portion of LCC that gets the most sun reaches from Mexican Crack to the Coffin. The high ridge to the south blocks most of the sun that reaches the Gate Buttress and environs in the winter months. In summer, for the climber chasing shadows, the Green Adjective Gully is good in the morning and The Dihedrals area is best in the evening. Another good summertime hangouts is the Pentapitch Area.

Ice climbing in the lower portion of the canyon deserves mention. Scruffy Band, an epithet that stuck, is just that—a smear of ice on the first granite outcrop on the south side of the canyon. It is intermediate to advanced territory, depending on ice conditions. The Great White Icicle, a superb five-pitch climb that is moderately difficult and almost always formed up, is 1.8 miles up canyon. It is entirely possible to go ice climbing, rock climbing and skiing on the same day without leaving the canyon.

The modern climbing scene is a far cry from the happy-go-lucky, carefree days when climbers were a small user group. Today, land ownership in LCC is an important consideration for anyone planning to enjoy the rock. The LDS church owns property that stretches, roughly, from below the church archives to up past the Gate Buttress. (Most remaining cliffs of interest to climbers belong to the Forest Service.) Unfortunately, too, parking is limited in LCC. Nonetheless, positive steps are being taken to preserve our crags. In 1984, a parcel of land in LCC was acquired by the Forest Service via a complex land exchange. In 1989, after the LDS Church posted No Trespassing signs, Ted Wilson and Rick Reese, representing the climbing community, successfully negotiated for continued access. Future climbing practices, in part determined by the courtesy and respect of regular users, potentially may be different from what this guidebook describes.

CAMPING In Little Cottonwood Canyon, the Tanner's Flat Campground always has been a favorite. It is 4.1 miles up LCC, costs $11/vehicle and has 38 sites available. Also in LCC is the Albion Basin Campground, at the absolute end of the road in the heart of the Alta ski resort. The first vehicle is $11 per night, with 26 sites available. This campground really cools off at night and is open only in the warmest months.

AMENITIES Two options exist depending upon which way you are travelling. From the mouth of the canyon, Highway 209 (see overview map, page 28) bends to become 9400 South and heads west towards Sandy. Along the north side of 9400 South at roughly 2000 East is a Smith's supermarket with a drive-through ATM, and an Amoco and 7-11 for gas, both with ATM machines. The second option from the mouth of the canyon is to follow Highway 210 north (Wasatch Blvd.) toward Salt Lake. At the corner of Wasatch Blvd. and 7800 South, turn left. One block west, at the corner of 7800 South and 3500 East is a Smith's supermarket and an ATM machine. Continuing north on Wasatch Blvd. toward Salt Lake brings you to the next intersection which is at the mouth of Big Cottonwood Canyon. A 7-11 here sells gas and has an ATM.

LITTLE COTTONWOOD BOULDERING

Climbers have been bouldering in Little Cottonwood Canyon for years. In fact, the most popular bouldering area, the Gate Boulders, have long been considered the hub of Wasatch rock climbing. Bouldering in the shade of the oaks on a summer evening, or working a problem surrounded by the changing colors of a crisp fall day, are as much a part of the local rock climbing experience as are the crack, face and knob routes on the cliffs above. Recently, local climbers have been exploring for new bouldering areas, often finding gold right off the side of the road. Below is a list of the most convenient bouldering areas in the canyon. All mileages are up-canyon distances from the "neon" information sign at the mouth of the canyon.

Area 1 The Secret Garden (0.2 mile)   Several high quality boulders are within 100 feet of the road, sheltered by a small grove of oak and maple trees. Additional bouldering can be found by following the path uphill to the infamous "Tiger" boulder. This area can also be accessed from the northeast corner of the bus stop parking lot.

Area 2 The Cabbage Patch (0.4 mile)   Two boulders 25 feet from the road but hidden by trees provide the bulk of the problems, while several more boulders uphill are worth checking out.

Area 3 Mile Five Boulders (1.1 miles)   Most of the bouldering is located on or around the prominent Split Boulder. However, several additional boulders are located just down the road and towards the stream.

Area 4 The Gate Boulders (1.25 miles)   Park at the prominent parking areas on either side of the road. This is the most heavily used bouldering area, and with a wide range of difficulties, mostly good landings, and toprope anchors on the largest boulder, its popularity is deserved. Follow the trail at the west end of the parking area up into the trees to reach the boulders.

Area 5 The Swamp Boulders (1.35 miles)   Walk across a suspended pipe that forms a bridge over the stream. Beyond the stream, continue on the pipe for another 50 feet, then hop off at a path,

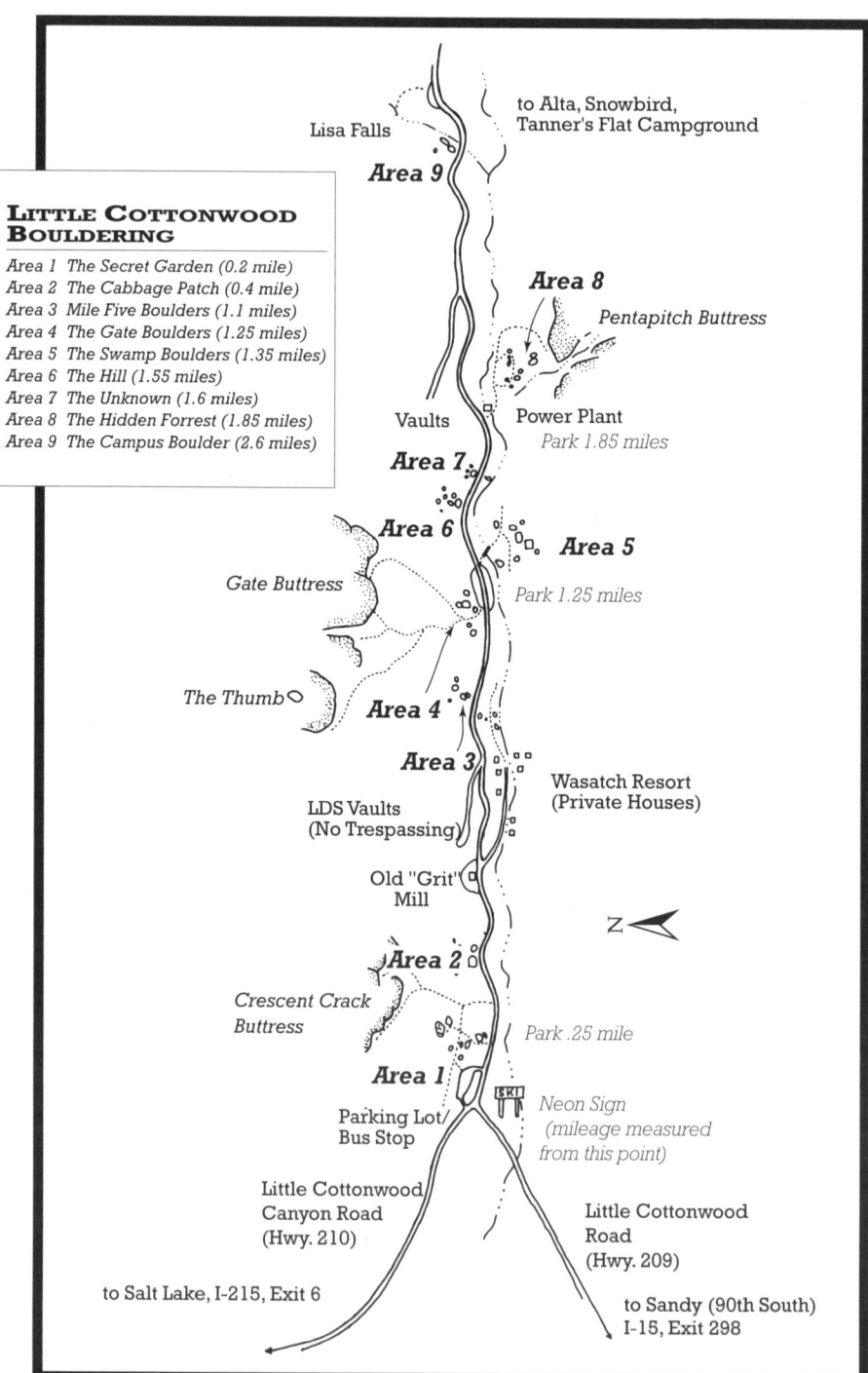

walk south, crossing another small stream, to an old pavilion. Boulders along the dirt road, both up and down canyon from here, are the attraction. These are the largest boulders in the area, and several of the rocks have bolts on top for anchors.

Area 6 The Hill (1.55 miles)   A large boulder is barely north of the road here, usually propped up (for a joke) with a spindly stick. This is a talus field, so there are a number of boulders, some of them are to the left in the trees.

Area 7 The Unknown (1.6 miles)   The east face of the boulder right off the road on the river side is the main attraction. Scattered bouldering on the uphill side of the road is also possible.

Area 8 The Hidden Forrest (1.85 miles)   Cross the river on the bridge and follow the path up canyon. This joins a wide trail which is followed east for several hundred feet to a stand of larger aspen trees. Just past these trees a small trail heads off right(south). Take this trail, hanging a left at the junction to the first of several scattered boulders. This area is in the pine trees and is a good choice for the warmer days.

Area 9 The Campus Boulder (2.6 miles)   A small stream flows past the boulders and crosses under the road. Only a dozen problems exist, but the stream adds a nice ambience.

CRESCENT CRACK BUTTRESS

The Crescent Crack Buttress is the first major rock formation on the north side of Little Cottonwood Canyon. The combination of varied climbing (usually less than vertical), reasonable approaches, and warm rock on sunny winter days make this area one of the canyon's main attractions.

APPROACH   Park .25 mile up canyon from the neon sign at the mouth of the canyon. A power line crosses the road here, and wooden steps lead northward up a bank of dirt and into the oak brush. Follow this trail as it meanders through the forest to an easy-to-miss fork in the trail. In the spring of 1996 a torrential downpour turned the trail into a streambed at this point, making this junction a bit hard to find. For routes 76 to 79, take the left (west) fork of the trail at the junction. Crescent Crack is reached after roughly one hundred and fifty feet of mostly level walking. It begins as a double crack system leading up and left into a deep chimney. For Mexican Crack (route number 78), continue up and left (west) on the trail for another one hundred and fifty feet to an alcove with a hand and finger crack that pinches down to a seam. For Crack in the Woods and Hand Jive (routes number 76 and 77),

CRESCENT CRACK BUTTRESS • LITTLE COTTONWOOD CANYON

CRESCENT CRACK BUTTRESS

76 Crack in the Woods (9) ★★
77 Hand Jive (8+) ★★
78 Mexican Crack (10a) ★★★
79 Crescent Crack (7) ★★
80 Exsqueeze Me (11d) ★★
81 The Coffin (9) ★★★
82 The Coffin Roof (12a) ★★★
83 The Viewing (10a) ★★★

Little Cottonwood Canyon • The Thumb

continue left (west), then up another one hundred and fifty feet to a chimney with a finger and hand crack on its right side.

To reach the Coffin Area (routes 80-83), continue straight up the wash from the trail junction mentioned above, joining the talus and gully descending from the Coffin. March up this until it is possible to scramble left (west) over some ledges and broken rock to reach the base of the Coffin. See canyon overview, page 28.

DESCENT   Single rope rappels work for all the routes in this area with the exception of Crescent Crack, which is descended by climbing a chimney above the final belay, then traversing east into the gully below the Coffin. This gully leads down to the trail junction described in the approach section.

- 76   **Crack in the Woods   (9)   ★★**   A #1 Friend eater.
- 77   **Hand Jive   (8+)   ★★**   Combine this with *Crack in the Woods*. Downclimb 10', stem, then gain a nice crack.
- 78   **Mexican Crack   (10a)   ★★★**   Top ten for sure.
- 79   **Crescent Crack   (7)   ★★**   A direct finish (not on topo) can be done by continuing up the crack above the ramp (5.9).
- 80   **Exsqueeze Me   (11d)   ★★**   Thin slab.
- 81   **The Coffin   (9)   ★★★**   Classic crack. Right side and left side second pitches are 5.9. Start in left seam (sparse pro.).
- 82   **The Coffin Roof   (12a)   ★★★**   Old style 5.12a. Down aid for descent.
- 83   **The Viewing   (10a)   ★★★**   Somewhat runout with awesome climbing. Start by climbing the *Coffin* for 25 feet, then traverse right at a black spot.

THE THUMB

This buttress is the largest in the canyon and is distinguished by the thumb-like pinnacle resting atop acres of clean granite. The S-crack, coupled with the S-direct, makes for a magnificent eight-pitch (nine, if the true summit is reached) route and is given a grade four rating. Many of the first ascents on the Thumb were climbed prior to 1970, yet even with modern equipment, they still feel committing, and require a full day.

APPROACH   The best view of the The Thumb, a large pinnacle-like formation on the left (north) side of the road, is at 1.05 miles up the road, at a bend in the road. However, the approach begins at the Gate Buttress parking area 1.25 miles up canyon from the neon sign at the mouth of the canyon.

As you approach the first boulder at the Gate Boulders, follow the path that leads left (west). The trail climbs up and west above the Tower Boulder,

THE THUMB

84	Indecent Exposure Variation (7)	★★
85	S-Crack III (8 A1, or 11d A0, or 12a)	★★
86	S-Direct II (9+ R)	★★★
87	Plumb Line (10a)	★★

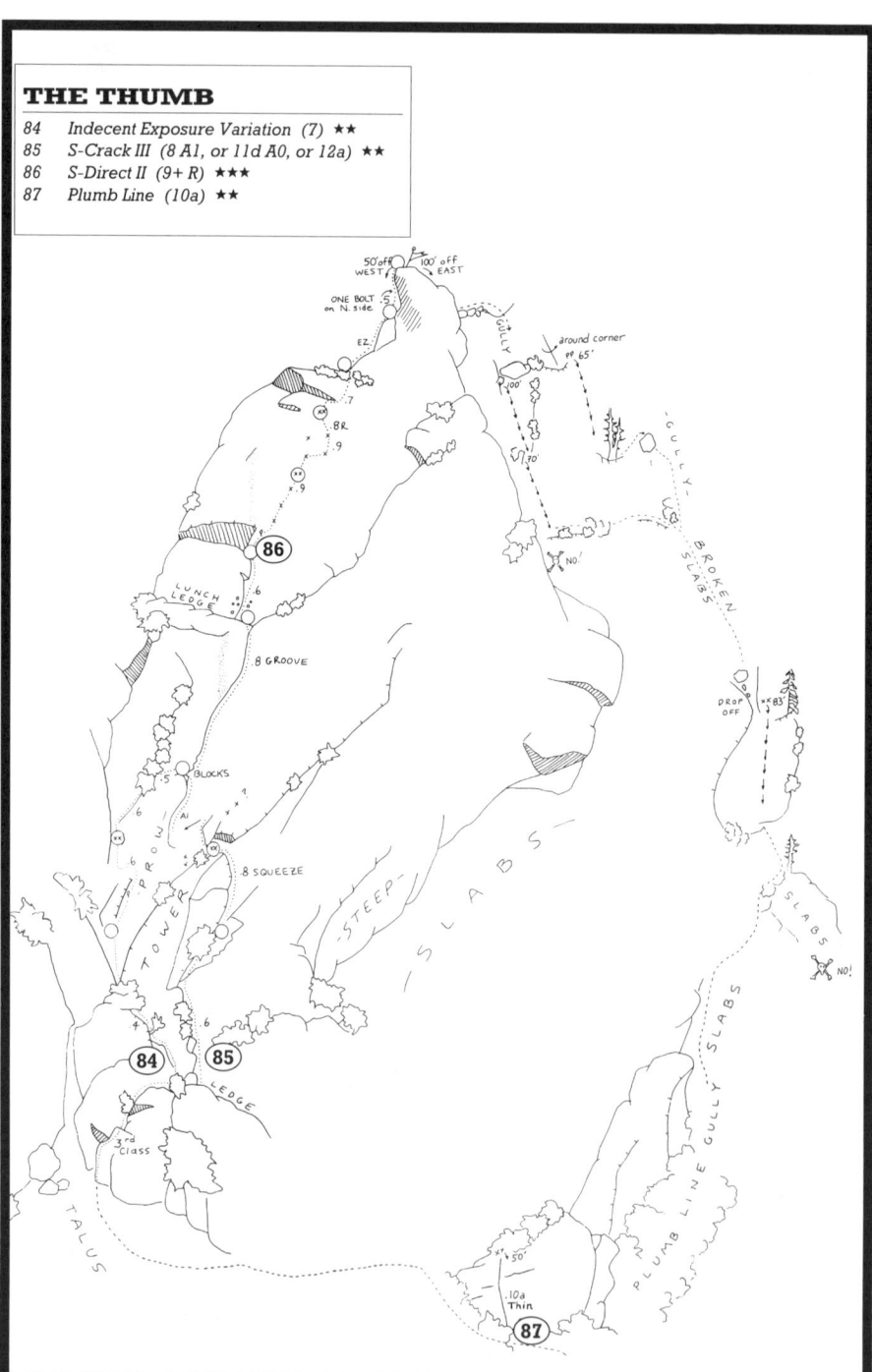

LITTLE COTTONWOOD CANYON • THE THUMB

along the base of a short slab. Take the lower fork here and follow the trail into the boulder field (see map, page 39). The trail crosses through the boulders, then continues up and west until it meets the base of the Waterfront. Keep traversing west, under the Waterfront. The trail then climbs up to the Plumb Line Wall. Many Thumb climbers stow their packs in this area, which alleviates the traverse back to the base of The Thumb from this point on the descent. Continuing to the Thumb, the trail climbs up and left (west) for one hundred and fifty feet, then traverses left (west) through the trees and below a slabby cliffband, to the gully at the base of the routes.

DESCENT *See descent drawing on topo on page 36. Two options exist for the first rappels. It is important to traverse into the gully at the bottom of the second rappel, if you choose the western option. On the eastern option, the two pin anchor is hidden around a corner on the north side of a ledge. Both descents eventually join and share an eighty foot rappel. Below that point, be careful not to miss the cut-off into the Plumb Line Gully.*

84 **Indecent Exposure Variation (7)** ★★ This variation avoids the chimney and aid on pitch two and three of the *S-crack*, traversing in to join the start of the exhilarating fourth pitch. Somewhat gritty rock.

85 **S-Crack (III 8 A1, or 11d A0, or 12a)** ★★ The second pitch can be protected by climbing a crack to the right of the chimney, protecting at its top, then downclimbing and tackling the chimney. The third pitch can be climbed several ways, the first possibility is rated A.1. Aid up the left facing corner for twenty feet, pendulum left, then aid up the S-crack to the belay. The second option is 5.11d A0. Free climb the left facing corner, pendulum left, then free climb to the belay. The final option is a 5.12a squeeker, that free climbs from the belay past two bolts directly to the bottom of the S-crack, then frees the crack to the belay. The fourth pitch is tricky to protect and wonderfully exposed.

86 **S-Direct (II 9+ R)** ★★★ Bold elegance in a sea of white granite. Take measures to minimize rope drag on the third, runout pitch.

87 **Plumb Line (10a)** ★★ A great fingertips-to-thin hand crack. Bring small wireds.

THE GATE BUTTRESS AREA

The Gate Buttress and surrounding areas are home to over one hundred and fifty routes, most of which offer excellent climbing in all the grades. As a result, the Gate Buttress is immensely popular. Numerous routes kick back at a comfortable angle, offering fine beginner terrain, but not at the exclusion of more extreme routes. There are plenty of those as well. The Gate Buttress is located 1.25 miles up canyon from the neon sign at the mouth of LCC.

The traditional gathering spot for climbers to boulder, meet partners, socialize and retreat from the summer heat is the Gate Boulders, at the base of the Gate Buttress. This verdant and shady area is home to boulders that seem designed to be climbed. In the middle of summer, it is still pleasant beneath the big oaks and maples that shade these boulders. In autumn, among the carpet of leaves, it is magic.

The entire Gate Buttress area is owned by the Church of Jesus Christ of Latter-Day Saints. This area has been the subject of enforced closures off and on over the past decade. These closures were primarily due to liability fears of church leaders, fears that result from the litigious nature of today's society. Climbers therefore are urged to use the utmost care when climbing on this private property and to take full responsibility for their actions. Please keep this area trash free, strive to reduce the environmental impacts, and be courteous to others. Remember, climbing here is a privilege, not a right.

APPROACH   All approaches depart from the boulders at the base of the Gate Buttress. Several separate climbing walls comprise the Gate Buttress Area, and specific approach information is included in the description of each area.

DESCENT   Almost all of the routes in this area require a rappel for the descent. Specific descent information is included in the description of each area, and on the topo, if possible.

KERMIT'S WALL AND PERHAPS AREAS

This slabby playground is located on the left most (west) abutment of the Green Adjective Gully. Being mostly south-facing and warm, this cliff is amiable for much of the year. Summer shade makes for great evening climbing.

APPROACH   As you approach the first boulder at the Gate Boulders, follow the path that leads left (west). The trail climbs up and west above the Tower Boulder, along the base of a short slab, to a slippery lieback between two boulders. Above this challenge, the trail continues straight up, then moves into the boulder field near the right (east) edge of a large slab. Traverse left (west) on ledges above the slab into the next boulder field. Walk directly up this talus, roughly paralleling the the buttress on the right, until several large

Little Cottonwood Canyon • The Gate Buttress Area

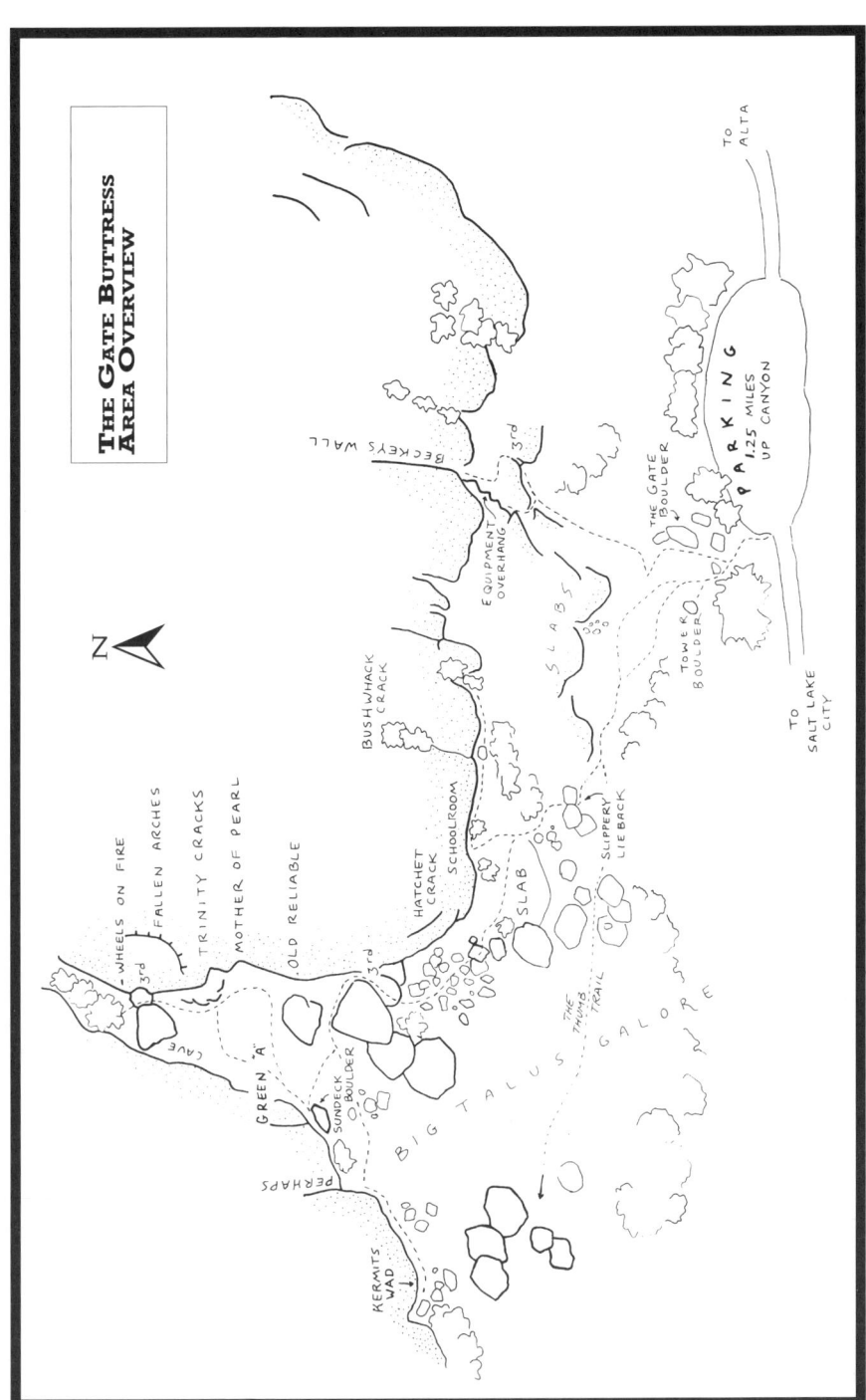

KERMIT'S WALL • LITTLE COTTONWOOD CANYON

KERMIT'S WALL

88 Paranoia Streak (10c R) ★★★
89 Koyaanisqaatsi (12c) ★★
90 Kermit's Wad (10a) ★★
91 Smitty's Wet Dream (9) ★★
92 Cranial Prophylactic (8) ★★

boulders form an impasse. Cracks and ledges on the right (east) wall of this impasse allow for some third class climbing to reach the top of the boulder. Walk directly across the top of this boulder, then straight up to reach the Sun Deck boulder at the base of The Green Adjective (route number 100). Or from the top of the boulder walk straight across more talus to reach the bottom of Perhaps (route number 95). From Perhaps, walk downhill through more talus to reach a flat spot at the base of Kermit's Wall. See overview map page 39.

DESCENT Single rope rappels work for all routes in this area with the exception of Paranoia Streak and Koyaanisqaatsi. For Paranoia Streak a single rope rappel is possible, but some downclimbing is involved. Koyaanisqaatsi requires two ropes or a downclimb to the anchors at the top of Paranoia Streak.

- 88 **Paranoia Streak (10c R)** ★★★   Healthy runouts. Bring gear up to 2 inches for the upper crack.
- 89 **Koyaanisqaatsi (12c)** ★★   Thin face final exam.
- 90 **Kermit's Wad (10a)** ★★   Great rock quality.
- 91 **Smitty's Wet Dream (9)** ★★   Slick rock and sequential moves.
- 92 **Cranial Prophylactic (8)** ★★
- 93 **All Chalk and No Action (12a)** ★★★   Clean, small edges on a vertical face.
- 94 **Touch Up (9+)** ★★   Pumper hand traverses.
- 95 **Perhaps (7)** ★★   Second pitch can have heinous rope drag; take precautions.
- 96 **Gordon's Hangover (9+)** ★★★   Thrilling lieback and jamming moves.
- 97 **Gordon's Direct (11b R)** ★★   Bring some RPs for the initial moves.
- 98 **MA #1 (10a)** ★★   Climbs hanging corner.>
- 99 **Meat Puppets (12b/c)** ★★★   Great position. Steep but less-than-vertical crux.
- 100 **The Green Adjective (9)** ★★★   Small nuts for first pitch. Impeccable granite.
- 101 **Dangling Participle (11a R)** ★★   A solid seconding climber is advised.

THE GREEN ADJECTIVE GULLY

This gully, with its shade and vertical walls, has a special character. In the summer, this gully provides hours of stupendous climbing before the sun strikes. Most of the routes here are steep–in fact, much steeper and more

LITTLE COTTONWOOD CANYON • GREEN ADJECTIVE GULLY   43

THE GREEN ADJECTIVE GULLY
102 Wheels on Fire (9) ★★
103 Fallen Arches (13a/b) ★★★

LITTLE COTTONWOOD CANYON • MAIN GATE BUTTRESS 45

continuous than most of the Gate Buttress. Therefore, the free climbing is some of the most difficult in the Wasatch.

APPROACH   Follow the approach description for the Kermit's Wall and Perhaps Area. At the Sun Deck boulder at the base of The Green Adjective route, a faint trail heads up the left (west) side of the gully. To approach the route Catalyst and environs, leave the trail after several hundred feet and cut across to the east side of the gully. Continue up the gully from Catalyst to reach the Trinity Cracks and Wheels on Fire. To reach the base of Wheels on Fire, a short section of water polished third class must be negotiated. See overview map on page 39.

DESCENT   It is possible to rappel off all the routes in this area with one rope with the exception of Mother of Pearl, which requires two ropes. However, many climbers use two ropes to rappel from the top of Nip and Tuck and Old Reliable. A scramble down to the top of the Schoolroom Rappel can also be made from the top of these two routes.

- 102 **Wheels on Fire (9)** ★★   Popular and highly recommended.
- 103 **Fallen Arches (13a/b)** ★★★   A third class ramp down-gully from *Wheels on Fire* seems to provide the quickest access to the base. The Wasatch crack test piece.
- 104 **Trinity Left (12d)** ★★★   An unequivocal pump!
- 105 **Trinity Center (13a)** ★★★   Gorilla climbing and bizarre sequences
- 106 **Trinity Right (12a)** ★★★   A lunge for the belay slings is common.
- 107 **Mother of Pearl (11c)** ★★★   Can be done in one, two, or three pitches. A few small nuts and/or RPs are handy, in addition to a standard rack.
- 108 **Looney Tunes (11b R)** ★★   A #3½ Friend protects the bold start.
- 109 **Badlands (12a)** ★★   Bring flexible legs.
- 110 **Catalyst (10c)** ★★   Rope drag seems inevitable.
- 111 **Nip and Tuck (12b/c)** ★★   Bring gear and expect hard, baffling moves.
- 112 **Old Reliable (10d R)** ★★   Poor protection at the beginning. Bold liebacking.

THE MAIN GATE BUTTRESS

This large chunk of granite is crossed by many excellent routes which link together cracks and slabs. Nubbins and crystals provide great friction on some routes while others, like Bushwhack Crack are perfect hand and finger cracks. Mostly south-facing, this wall basks in the sun, although mornings and evenings are fine, even in the heat of summer.

MAIN GATE BUTTRESS • LITTLE COTTONWOOD CANYON

THE MAIN GATE BUTTRESS

113 Hatchet Crack (7) ★★
114 Schoolroom West (7) ★★
115 Schoolroom (6) ★★★
116 Schoolroom Direct (7 R) ★★
117 Knobs to Gumbyland (10c) ★★
118 Mind Blow (10d) ★★
119 The Hook (8 R) ★★
120 The Hook Variation (7) ★
121 Bushwhack Crack (8) ★★
122 The Bungle (11a) ★★
123 Callitwhatyouplease (8) ★★

APPROACH *As you approach the first boulder at the Gate Boulders, follow the path that leads left (west). The trail climbs up and west above the Tower Boulder, along the base of a short slab, to a slippery lieback between two boulders. Above this challenge, the trail continues straight up then moves into the boulder field near the right edge of a large slab. Continue walking straight above the slab another two hundred feet to reach the base of Schoolroom. Routes 116 to 123 can be reached by walking right (east) along the base of the wall from Schoolroom. To reach Hatchet crack (route number 113), walk west on ledges above the previously mentioned slab to a boulder field. Walk up the talus until several huge boulders form an impasse. Cracks and ledges on the right (east) side allow for some third class climbing to reach the top of the boulder. Cutting right (east) behind a box elder tree and down climbing the ramp reaches the base of the route. See the overview map page 39.*

DESCENT *Use the Schoolroom Rappel for routes 113 through 117. From the pine tree atop Schoolroom, walk up and north, toward the Green Adjective Gully on a brushy ledge system to a pine tree. Either do one rappel off the pine or downclimb a crack and chimney to the ledge system below. Anchors here allow an eighty foot rappel to the ground. For climbs 118 through 123 it is best to utilize the Callitwhatyouplease Rappel. Both descents require some downclimbing to reach the anchors. Care should be taken. See topo for rappel locations, page 46.*

- 113 **Hatchet Crack** (7) ★★   Awkward bulges.
- 114 **Schoolroom West** (7) ★★   Lots of interesting climbing in five pitches.
- 115 **Schoolroom** (6) ★★★   Several pitches can be scary for the follower, if not protected properly by the leader.
- 116 **Schoolroom Direct** (7 R) ★★   The protection is not ideal.
- 117 **Knobs to Gumbyland** (10c) ★★   Sometimes wet. Mantle-o-rama.
- 118 **Mind Blow** (10d) ★★   Continuously difficult face climbing.

The following routes should use the Callitwhatyouplease tree rappel for descent.

- 119 **The Hook** (8 R) ★★   No bolts were used by the Klettershoe-laden first ascent party.
- 120 **The Hook Variation** (7) ★   A good friction alternative to *The Hook Crack*.
- 121 **Bushwhack Crack** (8) ★★   A great intro to true crack climbing.
- 122 **The Bungle** (11a) ★★   Two distinct cruxes; cool climbing.
- 123 **Callitwhatyouplease** (8) ★★   Bring protection to 3 inches.

THE DIHEDRALS AREA

Many of the routes in this area are steep corner and crack climbs. The rock is excellent, and the routes airy. With afternoon shade, these climbs are immensely popular.

APPROACH   To reach The Dihedrals and Tarzan areas, walk to the upper end of the Gate Boulder and follow a trail that leads left (west), then switchbacks east, before heading straight up through the trees. This path ends at twenty feet of third class climbing up a set of double cracks. Above the cracks, a short scramble leads to a ledge system and a traverse left (west). These ledges lead to a short gully and the base of Becky's Wall. A third class scramble up a short chimney near the base of Satan's Corner accesses the Dihedrals, routes 124 through 129. A short scramble right (east) from the gully accesses the belay bolt on Tarzan.

An easier alternative to reaching just the Dihedral Routes is to stop sixty feet before the slippery double cracks on the main trail, turn left (west) at a small break in the cliff band. From here, follow a ledge around the corner, and scramble up slabs to the base of the routes. See overview map page 39.

DESCENT   All routes can be descended with one rope. For Beckey's Wall routes, and Cheetah, scramble down to the large pine at the top of the Five Fingers Rappel. For Tingey's Terror, it is best to make a long scramble west to gain the Schoolroom Rappel. Some new bolts have recently been added to Beckey's Wall, for a swifter descent. See photo page 49.

- 124   **Half-a-Finger (9+)** ★★★   Strenuous and kind of bold.
- 125   **Black and White John and Mary (10c)** ★★★   The left start is common. Stemming and liebacking.
- 126   **Equipment Overhang (11a)** ★★★   The final 20 feet are a tickler. Superb.
- 127   **Equipment Overhang Right (10b)** ★★★   Thin crack with thin pro. at crux.
- 128   **Lisa's Shoulder (9 R)** ★★★   Climbs left face of upper corner. The upper face has bountiful thin holds and thin pro.
- 129   **Stem the Tide (10d R)** ★★   Three bolts up the corner proper. Runout but classic. Get psyched for this one.
- 130   **Satan's Corner (8)** ★★★   The best 5.8 in the canyon.
- 131   **Beckey's Wall (7)** ★★★   Climbs the huge right-facing dihedral. The start has somewhat tricky protection.
- 132   **Fingertrip Variation (8+ R)** ★★   RPs useful.
- 133   **Unknown (9)** ★
- 134   **Date With Fate (9)** ★

Little Cottonwood Canyon • The Dihedrals Area

THE DIHEDRALS AREA

124 *Half-a-Finger* (9+) ★★★
125 *Black and White John and Mary* (10c) ★★★
126 *Equipment Overhang* (11a) ★★★
127 *Equipment Overhang Right* (10b) ★★★
128 *Lisa's Shoulder* (9 R) ★★★
129 *Stem the Tide* (10d R) ★★
130 *Satan's Corner* (8) ★★★
131 *Beckey's Wall* (7) ★★★
132 *Fingertrip Variation* (8+ R) ★★
133 *Unknown* (9) ★
134 *Date With Fate* (9) ★★
135 *Cheetah* (11b R) ★★
136 *Tarzan* (10a) ★★
137 *Sweet Jane Variation* (7) ★
138 *Tingey's Terror* (7) ★★

135 **Cheetah (11b R)** ★★   Four pitches of knee-trembling slabwork.
136 **Tarzan (10a)** ★★   A classic crack climb with good protection.
137 **Sweet Jane Variation (7)** ★   An easier start to *Tarzan*.
138 **Tingey's Terror (7)** ★★   The longest offering at the Gate Buttress. Allow plenty of time for the descent to the Schoolroom Rappel.

THE PENTAPITCH AREA

The Pentapitch area is popular on summer mornings as it offers cool, northwest-facing climbing on good rock. Quality thin cracks split the slabs here, sometimes for a full pitch, other times linked together by face climbing. The rock is of a finer grain than most areas in Little Cottonwood Canyon and is reminiscent of Yosemite granite. The Pentapitch area is hard to see from the approach trail; however, it is the series of higher angled slabs just east (up canyon) from Coalpit Gulch and the ever pleasant Coalpit stream. See overview map, page 28.

APPROACH Park 1.85 miles up canyon from the neon sign at the mouth of the canyon (.6 miles up canyon from the Gate Buttress parking area). There is an old power plant here, as well as a bridge across the creek. Cross the bridge and walk up the trail to a junction with an old road/trail. Turn left (east) and walk up canyon on this trail for roughly one quarter mile (you will actually be past the Pentapitch Buttress). Look for a small path branching off right (south) just past two big pine trees and a flat spot. During runoff, a small stream here flows into a pipe underneath the main trail. Walk up the this path as it cuts through the trees and into a boulder field. Diagonal southwest across the boulder field, staying just above the trees, to a small drainage which is followed directly up to the base of Pentapitch. See canyon overview, page 28.

DESCENT Pentapitch can be descended via a series of five one rope rappels, or two 155 foot rappels.

139 **Endless Torment (10b)** ★★   An enjoyable two-pitcher.
140 **Pentapitch (II 8)** ★★★   Five (or fewer) pitches on excellent rock.
141 **Flashdance (11c or A1)** ★★   The original line. Bring RPs.
142 **Sasquatch (9+)** ★★★   This is one of the finest cracks in the canyon.

LITTLE COTTONWOOD CANYON • THE PENTAPITCH AREA

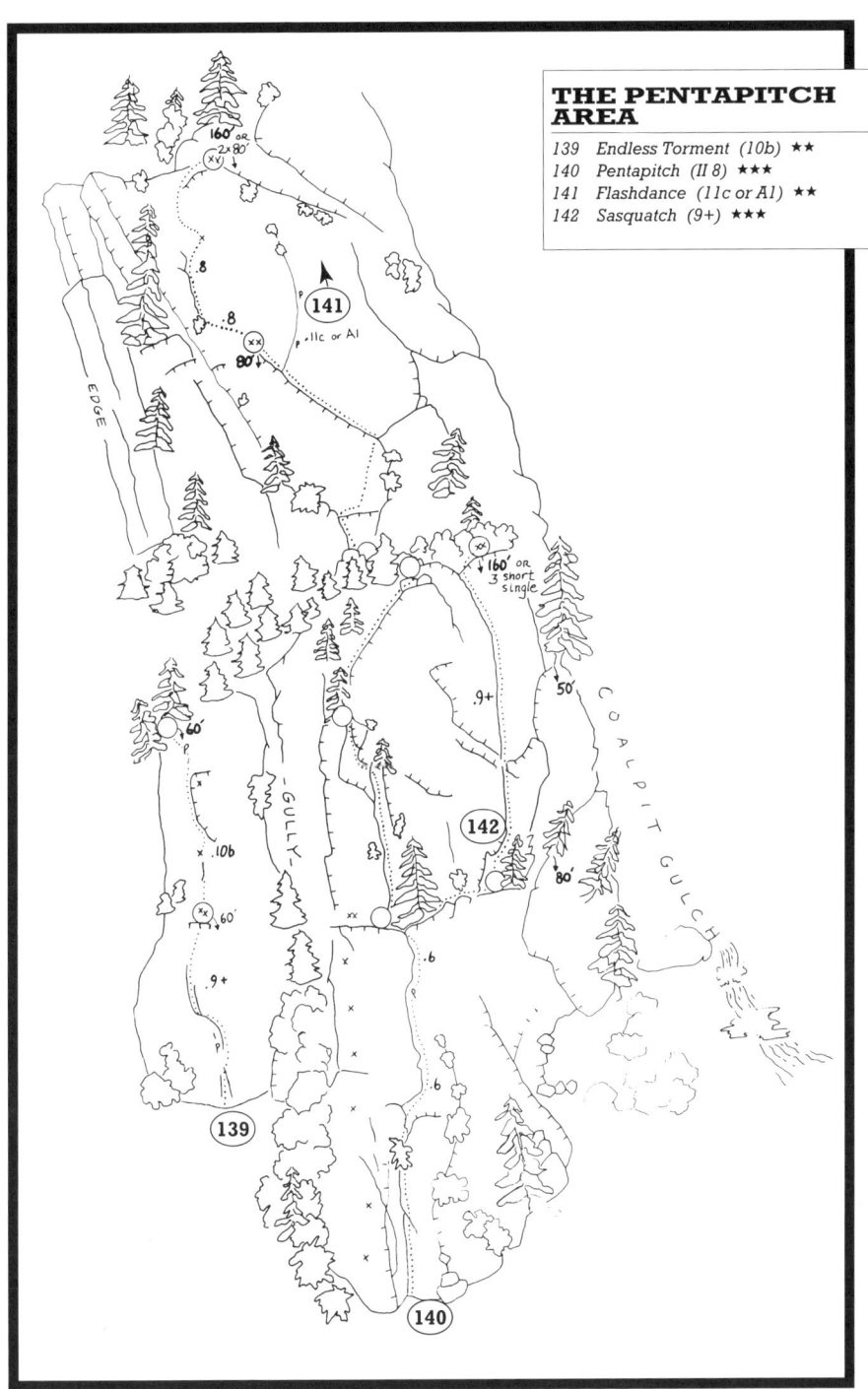

THE PENTAPITCH AREA

139 Endless Torment (10b) ★★
140 Pentapitch (II 8) ★★★
141 Flashdance (11c or A1) ★★
142 Sasquatch (9+) ★★★

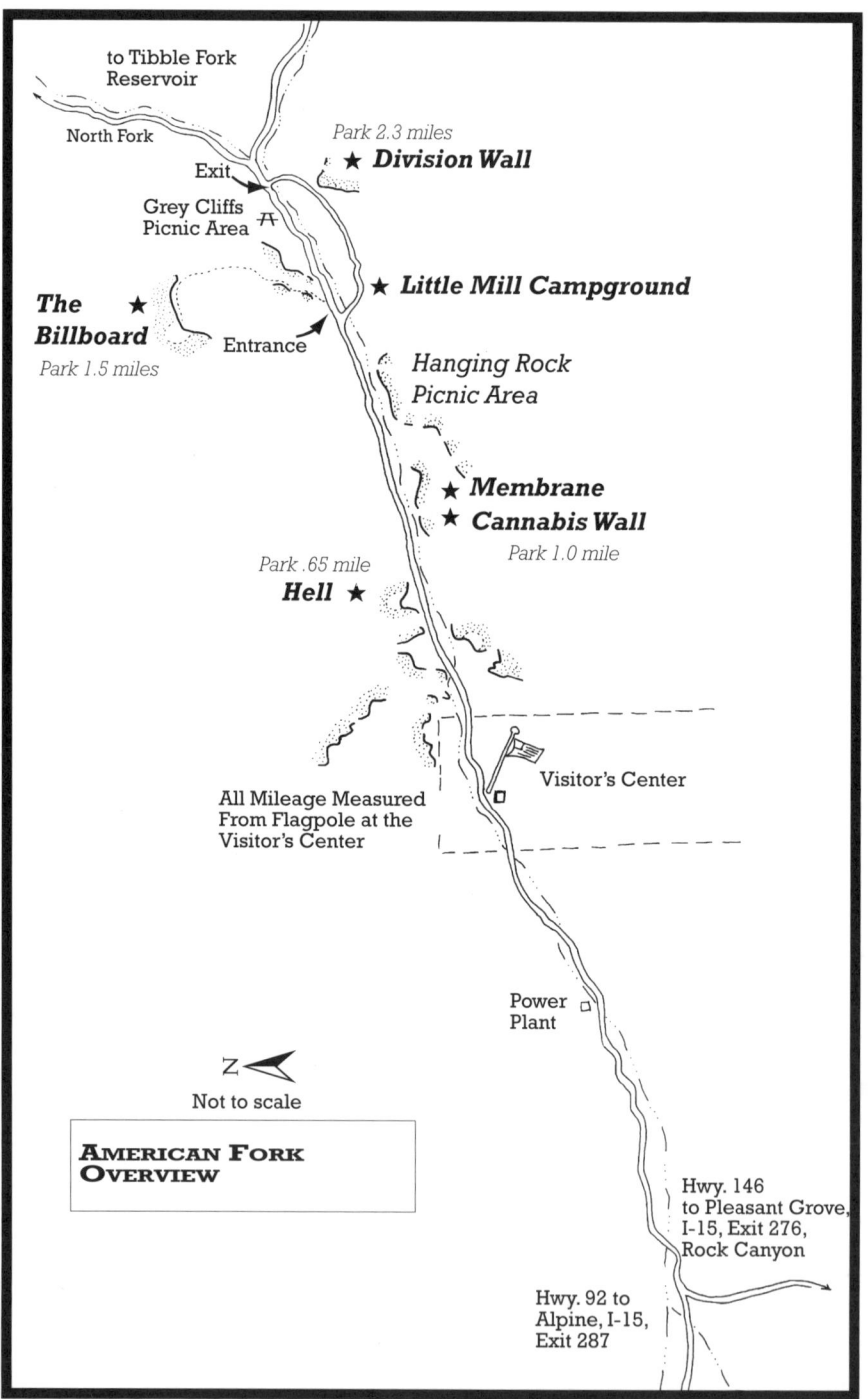

CHAPTER 3

AMERICAN FORK CANYON

The American Fork Canyon is a modern sport climbing area, featuring steep, challenging and innovative bolted routes. It has received widespread attention in the climbing community, and locals have worked diligently to expand the variety and quality of climbs. It is a beautiful canyon, lush with foliage, cool in the summer, and rugged with rock. The canyon cuts through the Wasatch range from the town of American Fork to the alpine slopes of Mt. Timpanogos.

HOW TO GET THERE From the north, take exit 287 off Interstate 15. This is the Alpine/Highland /Timpanogos Cave exit, and is located just south of "Point of the Mountain"—the gravel ridge separating Salt Lake Valley from Utah Valley. Once off I-15, drive east on Utah Highway 92; simply stay on it and you will drive directly into American Fork Canyon.

Joe Brooks on *Linus* (13c)

From the south, take exit 276 off Interstate 15. This is the Pleasant Grove exit. Turn right and drive east towards the mountains. Turn left on State Street. Drive north on State Street to an easy-to-miss intersection with Highway 146 (100 East). Turn right on 146 and follow this road all the way to the mouth of American Fork Canyon, where it joins Highway 92.

All mileage in American Fork Canyon is referenced from the flagpole at the Timpanogos Cave National Monument (TCNM). As of this writing, an entrance fee for entering the canyon is being debated.

CAMPING   In American Fork Canyon there is free and unimproved camping (at the time of this writing) in the North Fork of American Fork Canyon along the dirt road above and north of Tibble Reservoir. To get there, drive up American Fork Canyon (state road 92) until the road forks. Take the left fork (North Fork) towards Tibble Reservoir. Slightly less than four miles up the road, at a switch back above the reservoir, a dirt road leads off to the right (east). Follow this dirt road until signs indicate that unimproved camping is permitted (about .3 mile). Many choice sites exist. Of course, this could all change if climbers start trashing the area. For a fee of $11.00 per night there are plenty of campsites located in Little Mill Campground (located 1.3 miles up canyon from the TCNM flagpole). Additional camping is also available at four walk-in campgrounds along the North Fork road, at a fee of $13.00 per night.

AMENITIES   The nearest gas station is the Kountry Korner Chevron, located at the intersections of 1100 North and 5300 West (Highways 92 and 74). Kohler's, right across the street is the nearest supermarket and Bank of American Fork, just west of Kohler's, has a drive-thru ATM.

Pets are allowed in American Fork Canyon, unlike the Cottonwood Canyons.

HELL AREA

The Hell Area, destination for many of the world's finest rock climbers, is a dark cave with two radically overhanging flanks. Once dismissed as impossible, Hell now sports the greatest concentration of difficult routes in Utah. Even with the dramatic increase in climbing standards recently, Hell is still one of the most challenging areas in the United States.

The cave is known to non-climbers and Provo teenagers as Dance Hall Cave, and it is easy to imagine the partying that has taken place in this eerie spot. Now, with large bolts, quickdraws dangling, and climbers contorting themselves overhead, the atmosphere is vastly different. Big holds abound—pockets, edges, sidepulls—holds which require unique body positions. Climbing here is often a horizontal experience. The cave has bred a microcosm of mutant climbers, able to hang upside down for preposterous periods of time. Most climbers are hesitant when they first enter Hell, but if you're in a hurry to get strong, there is no better place to go. The Devil's price for a redpoint is steeeep!

APPROACH Park at the Hell parking area .65 mile up canyon from the TCNM flagpole. At the lowest point of the parking area (west end), cross the road and walk down canyon twenty feet. A trail here heads north, winds up a slope and ends at the hidden Hell Cave. See the Canyon Overview, page 52.

THE HELL WALL

This wall forms the west flank of the Hell Cave. A popular boulder traverse begins at Hell and moves up-slope to Jitterbug Boy (V 7/8).

DESCENT All routes in the Hell area can be lowered off with one rope.

143 **The Church of Skatin (12b/c)** ★   Climbs out of the alcove up to a boulder problem crux.

144 **Project**

145 **Romeo's Bleeding (11b)** ★   The climbing doesn't end at *Guillotine*'s anchors, but continues up past two more bolts to a higher set of chains.

146 **Guillotine (12d)** ★★   A bouldery, less difficult version of *Hell*.

147 **Hell (13a/b)** ★★★   A barrage of strange sequences.

148 **High Water (13c)** ★★   Join the upper portion of *Hell*.

149 **Higher Water (Variation) (14a)** ★★   Climb the boulder traverse beginning under Hell and moving rightward to join and finish *High Water*.

150 **Project**

151 **The Blight (12a)** ★   Small edges and a hard clip.

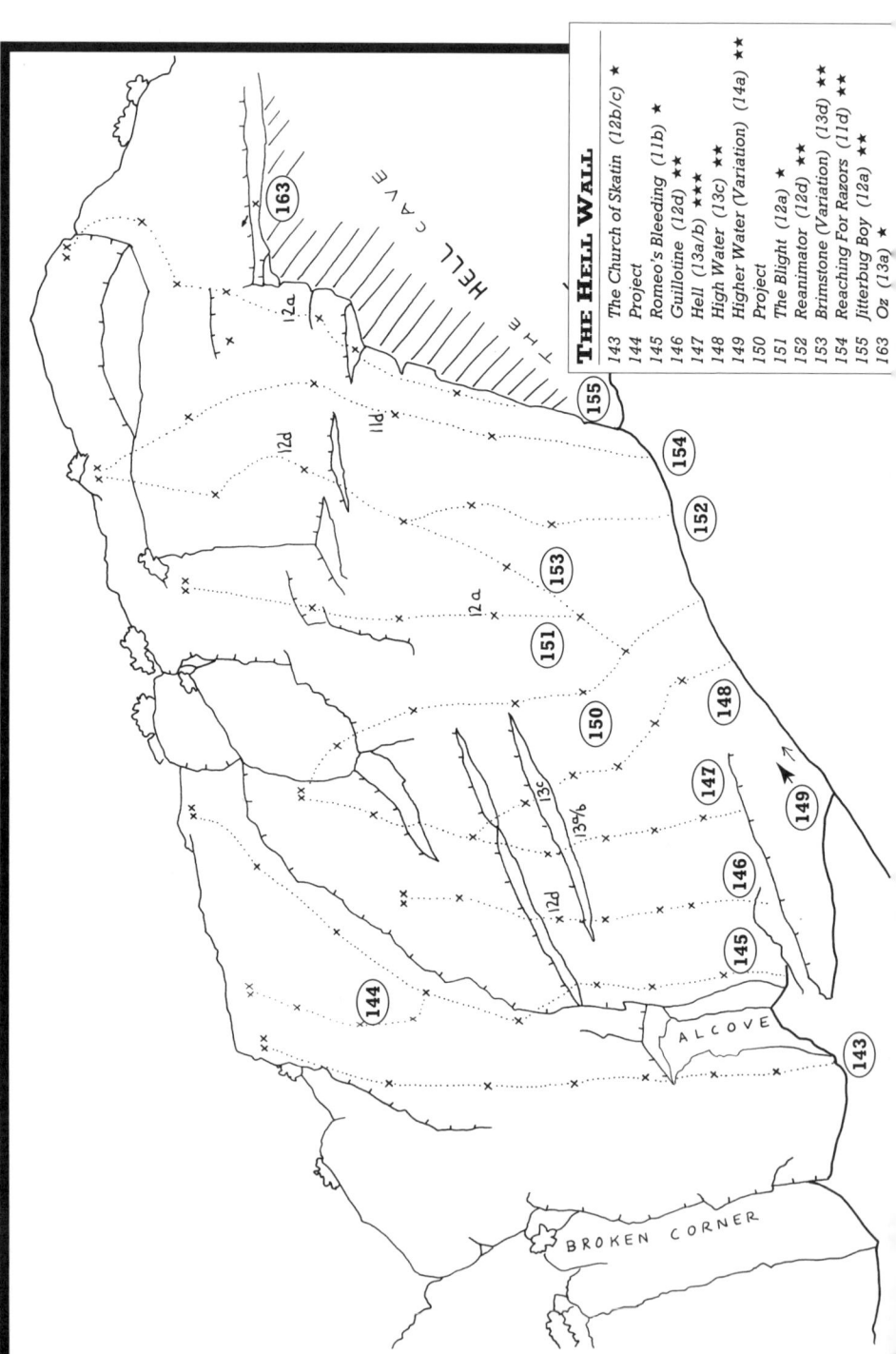

AMERICAN FORK CANYON • EL DIABLO WALL

152 **Reanimator (12d)** ★★ A crash coarse on crimpers.
153 **Brimstone (Variation) (13d)** ★★ Start at the boulder traverse beginning under *Hell*. Traverse rightward through the first and second bolts of *The Blight*, up past a new bolt to join *Reanimator* at its third bolt. Finish on *Reanimator*.
154 **Reaching For Razors (11d)** ★★ Crimpy and popular.
155 **Jitterbug Boy (12a)** ★★ A rightward amble of contorting moves.

HELL CAVE

This dark, moody cave is home to two boulder traverses that are worthy of note. The Peace, Dog, Beer Traverse begins under Linus and climbs rightward to the stem at the very back of the cave (V8) The Fuck Me traverse, named after the graffiti it crosses, starts at Cannibals and moves up slope to Wizards (V4).

156 **Wasatch Reality (12a)** ★ Stroll up the ungainly crack. Sharp.
157 **Burning (13b)** ★★★ Moves out a shelf to join *Wasatch Reality*. Shuffle right for two more bolts to clip the fixed carabiners.
158 **Linus (13c)** ★★ Cross *Burning* and finish on *Wasatch Reality*'s fourth bolt.
159 **Fryeing (13c)** ★★★ After the sixth bolt on *Burning*, cut right to the seventh bolt of *Cannibals*, and keep sizzling through the crux of *Wizards*. Finish on *Bats Out Of Hell*.
160 **Project (14?)**
161 **Cannibals (13d/14a)** ★★★ Ignore the jug at the sixth bolt on *Burning*, and pull the *Bats Out Of Hell* roof.
162 **Melting (12d/13a)** ★★★ Climb up *Wizards* to the third bolt, angle left to the fifth protection bolt on *Cannibals*, continue left to the eighth bolt on *Burning* and finish on *Burning*.
163 **Oz (13a)** ★ Climb *Melting* to the wide undercling. Traverse left past four bolts to the top of *Reaching For Razors*.
164 **Wizards (13b)** ★★★ Taping for the handjams is common.
165 **Bats out of Hell (12d)** ★ Choose your route to the *Wizards* anchor, then continue past two more bolts.
166 **I Scream (14?)** Open project. Have at it!
167 **Side Show Bob's (13b/c)** ★★ Stick clip the second bolt.

EL DIABLO WALL

This wall is the eastern continuation of the Hell Cave, and is the first wall encountered on the approach.

168 **Power Junkie (13d)** ★★★ 15 moves of power endurance.

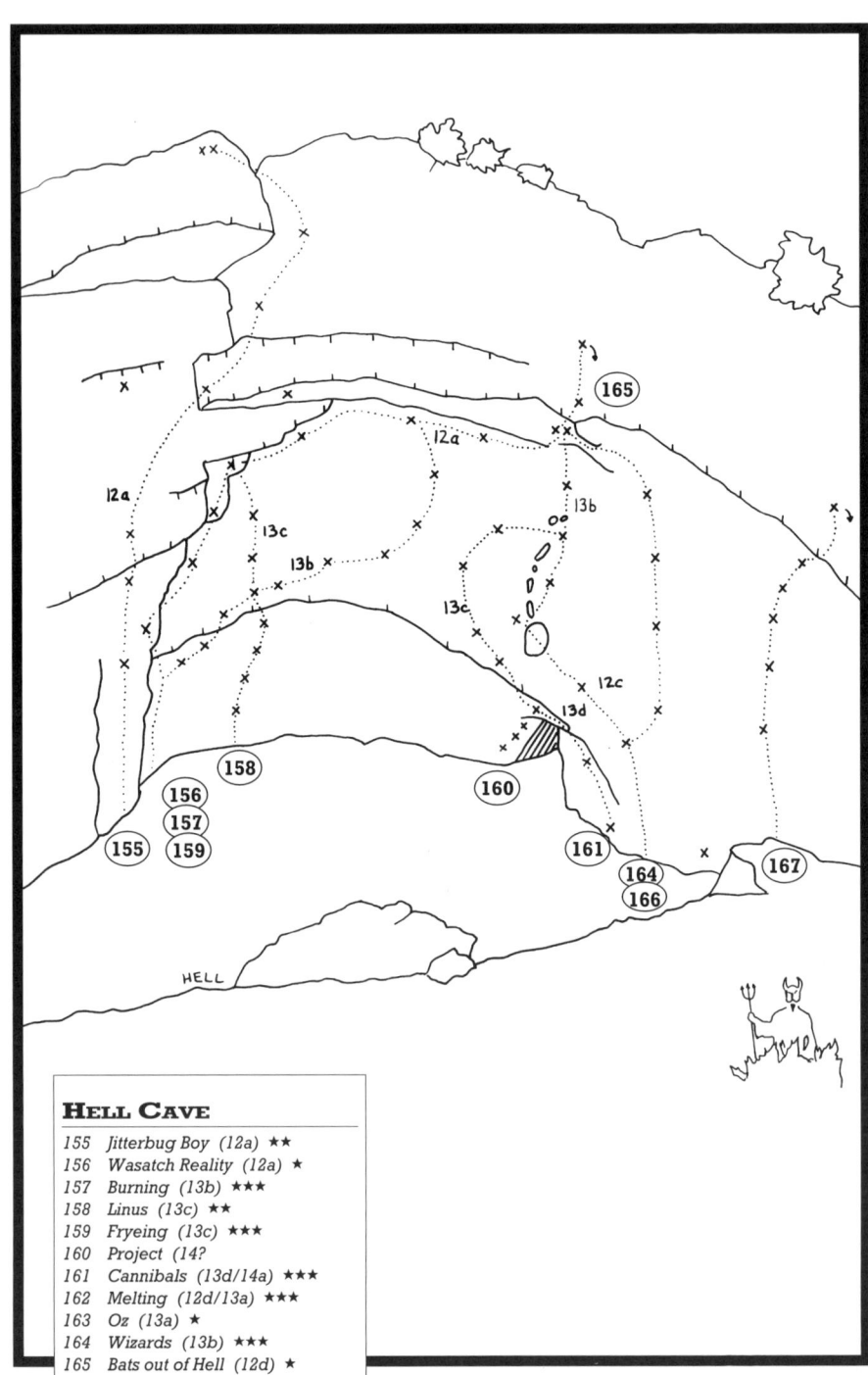

HELL CAVE

155 Jitterbug Boy (12a) ★★
156 Wasatch Reality (12a) ★
157 Burning (13b) ★★★
158 Linus (13c) ★★
159 Fryeing (13c) ★★★
160 Project (14?
161 Cannibals (13d/14a) ★★★
162 Melting (12d/13a) ★★★
163 Oz (13a) ★
164 Wizards (13b) ★★★
165 Bats out of Hell (12d) ★
166 I Scream (open project) (14?)

American Fork Canyon • El Diablo Wall

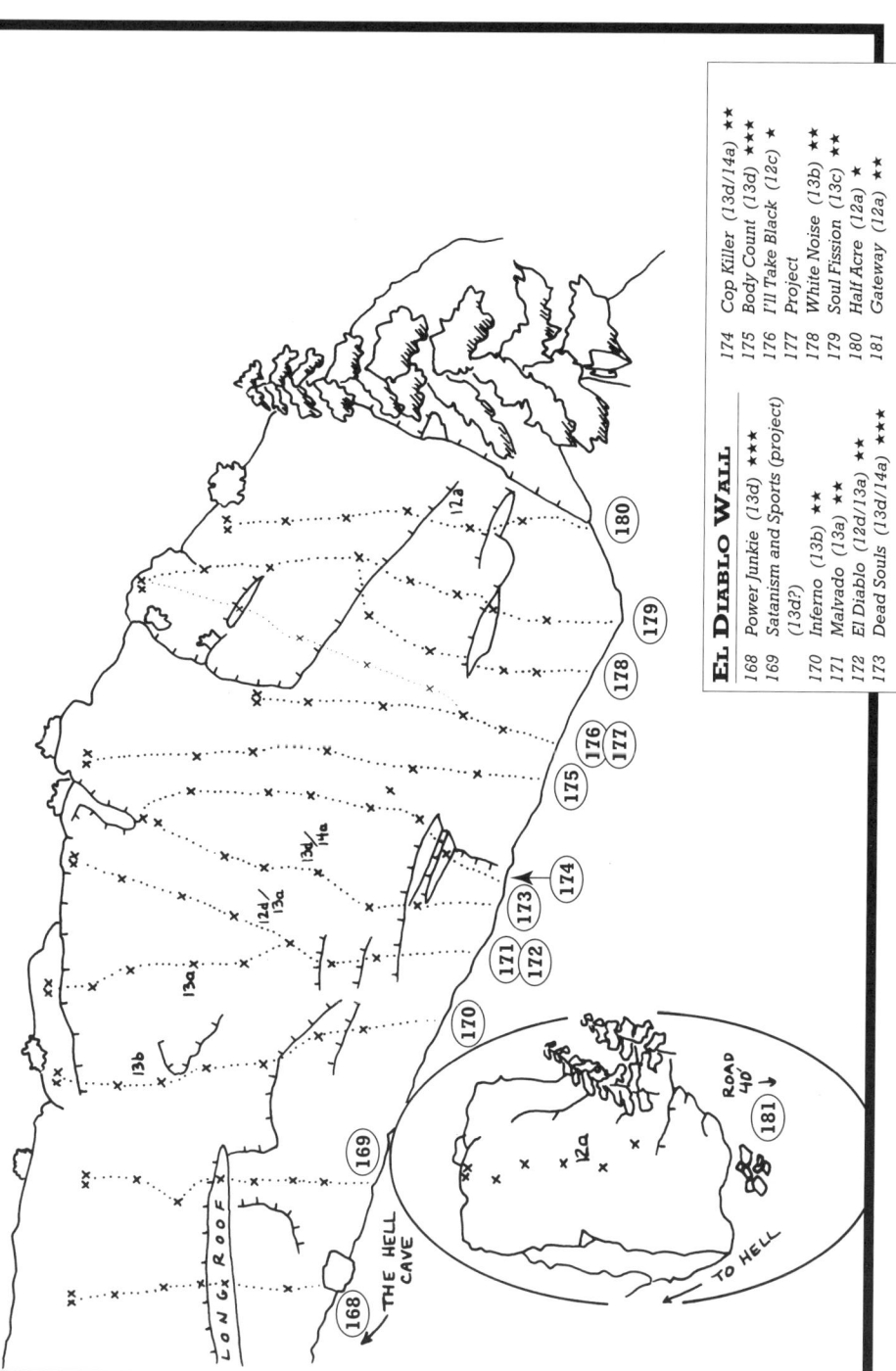

El Diablo Wall
- 168 Power Junkie (13d) ★★★
- 169 Satanism and Sports (project) (13d?)
- 170 Inferno (13b) ★★
- 171 Malvado (13a)
- 172 El Diablo (12d/13a) ★★
- 173 Dead Souls (13d/14a) ★★★
- 174 Cop Killer (13d/14a) ★★
- 175 Body Count (13d) ★★★
- 176 I'll Take Black (12c) ★
- 177 Project
- 178 White Noise (13b) ★★
- 179 Soul Fission (13c) ★★
- 180 Half Acre (12a) ★
- 181 Gateway (12a) ★★

169 **Satanism and Sports (13d?)** Project.
170 **Inferno (13b)** ★★ Highly creative climbing.
171 **Malvado (13a)** ★★ *El Diablo*'s more sinister twin.
172 **El Diablo (12d/13a)** ★★ Well traveled. Powerful underclings and small edges.
173 **Dead Souls (13d/14a)** ★★★ A wicked fusion of dead points and small crimps.
174 **Cop Killer (13d/14a)** ★★ Perhaps the hardest crux move in the canyon.
175 **Body Count (13d)** ★★★ A "long" journey to those close-looking chains.
176 **I'll Take Black (12c)** ★ Small edges, big pulls.
177 **Project**
178 **White Noise (13b)** ★★ Stick clip the second bolt. No single crux move.
179 **Soul Fission (13c)** ★★ Crimpfest.
180 **Half Acre (12a)** ★ There are many acres of slopers on this bulging plot.
181 **Gateway (12a)** ★★ The first route encountered on the approach, this faces south, about fifty feet from the road.

CANNABIS WALL

Shady and cool, the Cannabis Wall supplies an array of climbs ranging from the moderate in difficulty to the desperate. The routes here are characterized by powerful yet technical climbing. With few pockets, tenuous holds abound. See canyon overview page 52.

APPROACH   Park 1.0 mile up canyon from the TCNM flagpole on the right. Walk down canyon 200 ft., cross the stream, and the cliff will be staring you in the face. A high-water approach is possible, but more involved. Park .85 mile up canyon from the TCNM flagpole at a pullout. Walk down a trail to a pipe bridge that crosses the stream. Cross the bridge, turn left and head up canyon, paralleling the stream. Several dicey sections are encountered when brush forces the path of least resistance down to the edge of the water. This can be avoided by thrashing up an embankment and into the pine trees above. Continue heading up canyon, until a cliff band is reached which requires a careful traverse on a ledge system over the stream, ending, finally, at the Cannabis Wall.

DESCENT   It is possible to lower off chains at the top of each route in this area with a single (50m) rope.

182 **Sesame Street (11b)** ★★ No obvious crux.
183 **Electric Company (11b)** ★★ Shockingly good.

American Fork Canyon • Cannabis Wall

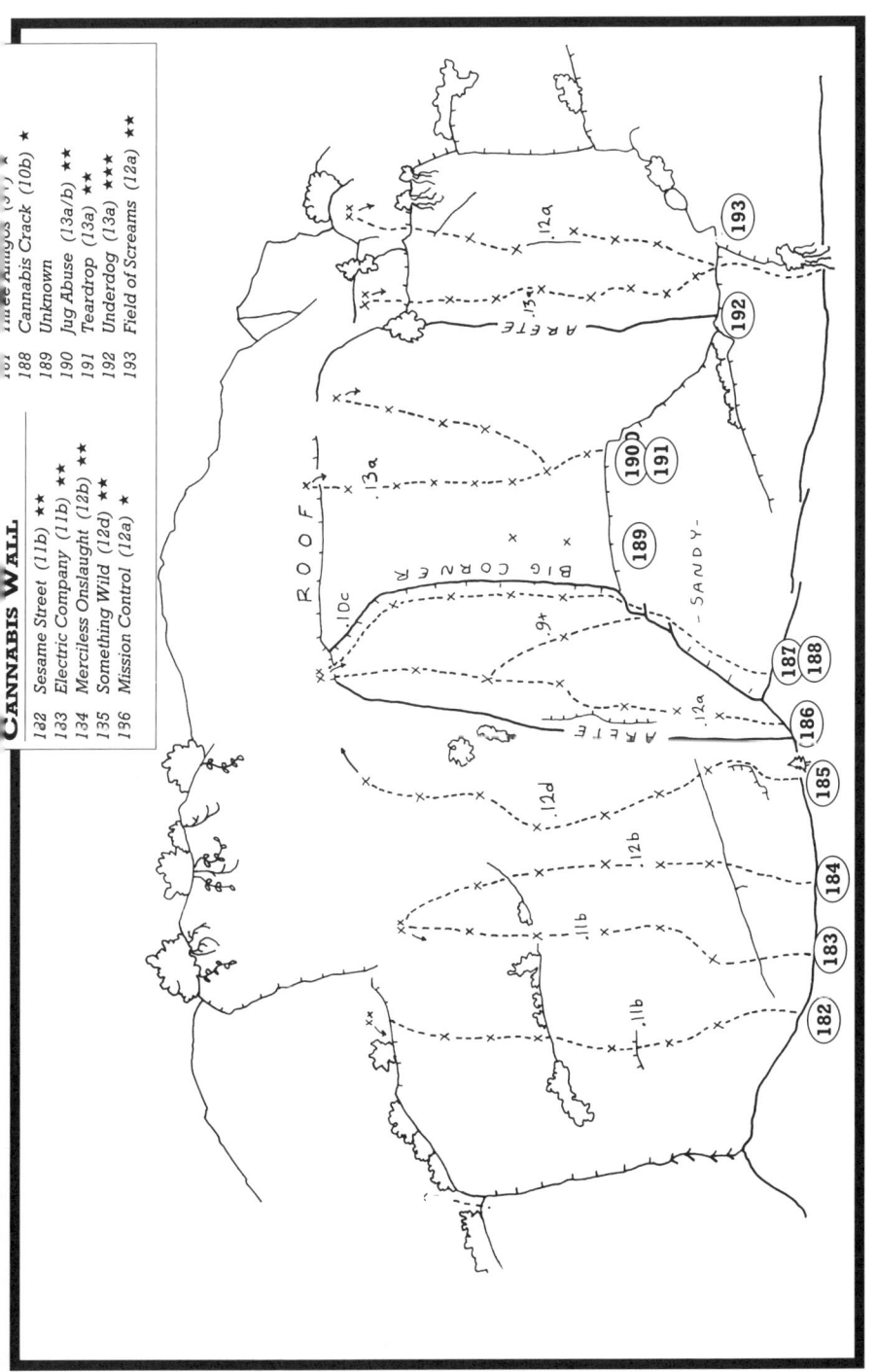

Cannabis Wall

- 182 Sesame Street (11b) ★★
- 183 Electric Company (11b) ★★
- 184 Merciless Onslaught (12b) ★★
- 185 Something Wild (12d) ★★
- 186 Mission Control (12a) ★
- 187 Three Amigos (*) ★
- 188 Cannabis Crack (10b) ★
- 189 Unknown
- 190 Jug Abuse (13a/b) ★★
- 191 Teardrop (13a) ★★
- 192 Underdog (13a) ★★★
- 193 Field of Screams (12a) ★★

184 **Merciless Onslaught (12b)** ★★ The name describes the difficulties.
185 **Something Wild (12d)** ★★ Beguiling moves up nothingness.
186 **Mission Control (12a)** ★ Bouldery crux moves right off the ground.
187 **Three Amigos (9+)** ★
188 **Cannabis Crack (10b)** ★ Kind of runout.
189 **Unknown** 2 bolts.
190 **Jug Abuse (13a/b)** ★★ Sophisticated power moves lead to an abusing finish.
191 **Teardrop (13a)** ★★ Move right at the second bolt.
192 **Underdog (13a)** ★★★ A tweak-fest up the right side of an arête.
193 **Field of Screams (12a)** ★★ The fourth clip is hard. Good climbing.

THE MEMBRANE

One of the most popular walls in American Fork Canyon, The Membrane has almost instant access, and steep climbing on edges and killer pockets. The northern exposure makes The Membrane cool even on the hottest days. In the spring, however, the pockets can sometimes be wet. Though frequently crowded, these routes are some of the canyon's finest. See canyon overview, page 52.

APPROACH Park 1.0 mile up canyon from the TCNM flagpole at a large pullout. At the upper end of the parking area, a trail leads down to the stream. Cross the stream on a telephone pole and you are at the Membrane. A hand line that helps to balance on the telephone pole seems to appear and then disappear with some frequency.

DESCENT It is possible to lower off chains at the top of each route in this area with a single (50m) rope.

194 **Little Big Wall (11d)** ★ Short, with a devious bulge.
195 **Unknown Project**
196 **Bad Faith (9)** ★
197 **Caress of Steel (10a)** ★★★ Classic jug-haul.
198 **Steel Monkey (10d)** ★★ Big pockets and one big reach.
199 **Route 66 (12a)** ★★ Finger buckets and stumper roof sequences.
200 **License to Thrill (11c)** ★★★ One of AFs best. Do it!
201 **Flight Fright (12c)** ★ Finish on *License to Thrill*.
202 **Mandela (12a)** ★★ Stems and sloper holds.
203 **Riptide (11a)** ★★ Steep climbing to an exciting final prow.

American Fork Canyon • The Membrane

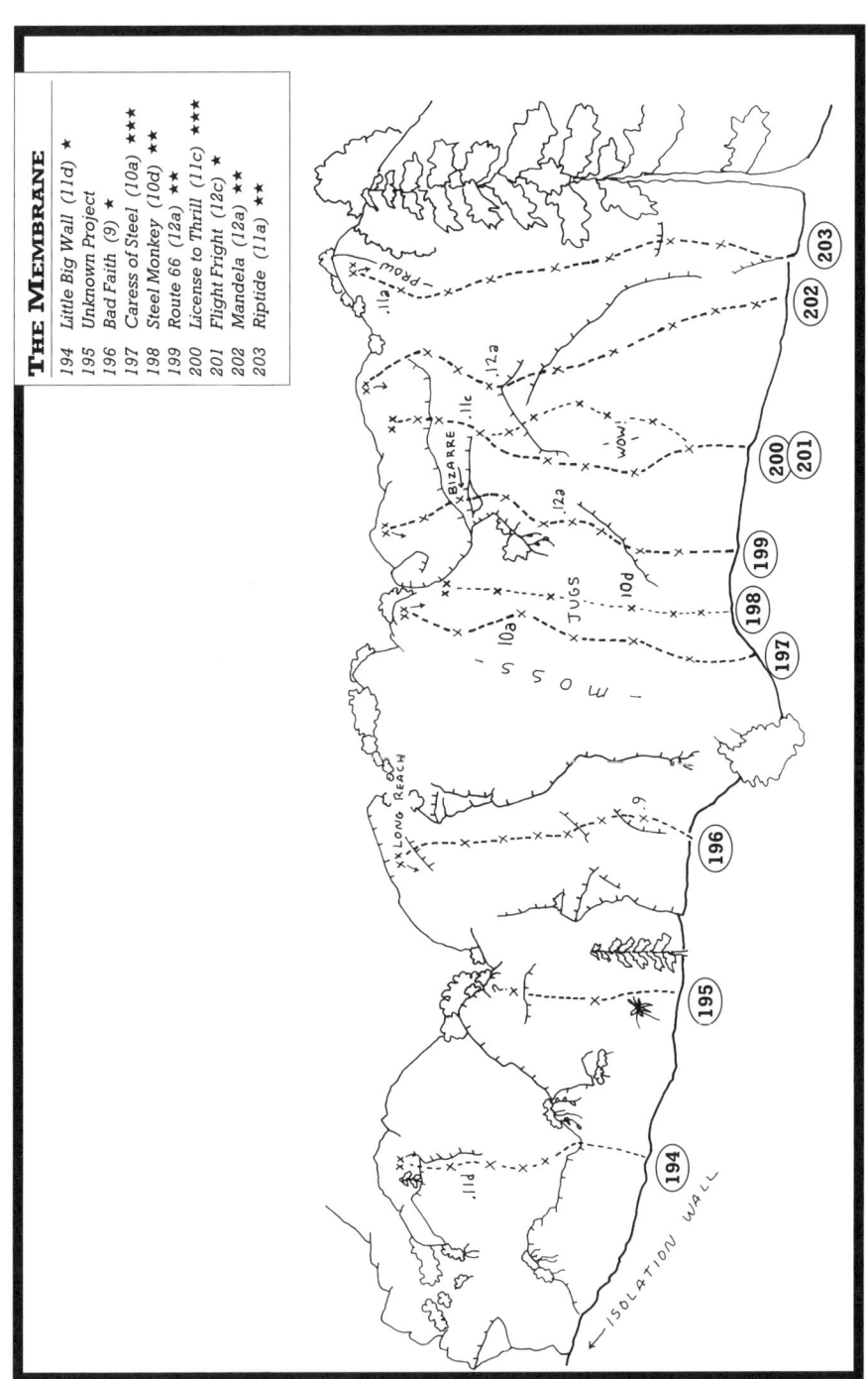

The Membrane

194 Little Big Wall (11d) ★
195 Unknown Project
196 Bad Faith (9) ★
197 Caress of Steel (10a) ★★★
198 Steel Monkey (10d) ★★
199 Route 66 (12a) ★★
200 License to Thrill (11c) ★★★
201 Flight Fright (12c) ★
202 Mandela (12a) ★★
203 Riptide (11a) ★★

THE BILLBOARD

With spectacular views of North Timpanogos and loads of hard climbs, The Billboard is possibly the finest crag in American Fork. It faces south and sits high on the north side of the canyon, creating an ideal winter training ground. However, it is also comfortable in mid-summer before noon on The Gridwall as it is all day long in The Shining Cave. The Gridwall tips to 100 degrees and has bolt spacing a bit more sporty than other areas in the canyon. The Shining Cave and Appetizer Wall offer much steeper climbing. During the first year of activity at The Billboard, a crude topo of the climbs was drawn on a large piece of canvas and stashed in The Shining Cave. Faded and torn, it remains in the archive today, its hidden treasures waiting to be unrolled.

APPROACH Park 1.5 miles up canyon from the TCNM flagpole at a small pullout on the right (south) side of the road(.2 mile up canyon from the entrance to Little Mill Campground). There is limited parking here, so continue up to the next pullout if the lower lot is full. From the lower area, cross the road and walk 100 feet up canyon to a small cairn at the base of an east diagonaling trail. The trail leads steeply up to the cliff from here. This hike takes about 30-40 minutes and is virtually impossible to describe, so stay on the trail. One comment: the trail tends to always go up and right. See page 52.

DESCENT It is possible to lower off chains at the top of every route with a single rope except for Gridlock, where a 55m rope is needed.

Routes 204 through 208 are located on the slightly overhanging Appetizer Wall.

- 204 **Gorillas in the Snow (12b)** ★★ Slopey, bouldery crux.
- 205 **Appetizer (12)** ★★★ Excellent package deal.
- 206 **Monkey Brains (13a)** ★★★ A techno-powerful line with small edges.
- 207 **Ghostdance (13b/c)** ★★ Continuous.
- 208 **The Final Sound (13a/b)** ★★ Bouldery moves guard the chains.

Routes 209 through 227 are located on the flanks or inside The Shining Cave.

- 209 **Fang (11c)** The crack bites at the top.
- 210 **Project**
- 211 **The One (12a)** ★ Unique crab-like climbing.
- 212 **The One That Got Away (12b/c)** ★★ The direct finish to *The One*.
- 213 **Eating the Gun (12d)** ★★ Bring a salvo of guns for this one.
- 214 **Red Rum (13b)** ★★★ Your fists will be screaming murder. A great route.

215 **Blue Murder (13c)** ★★★ Go right at *Red Rum's* 4th bolt.
216 **Project**
217 **Crack Baby (13a)** ★★ Climbs almost like a granite route.
218 **The Hard Blues (14a)** ★★★ A wicked direct start to *Blue Mask*.
219 **Blue Mask (13c)** ★★★ A roof problem that stands as a paragon.
220 **Invisible Man (13b/c)** ★★★ Begin on *Blue Mask*. Head straight up from its 8th bolt and climb past two more, then go left.
221 **Atmosphere (13a)** ★★★ Begin on Blue Mask. Head straight up at its 8th bolt.
222 **The Shining (13c)** ★★★ Climb straight up from the fourth bolt of *Blue Mask*.
223 **This Must be the Pickle (12d/13a)** ★★ Roofs, pockets and several wild sequences.
224 **Ambush (12a/b)** ★★ Crosses *The Whining*.
225 **The Whining (12a)** ★ Left arching crack and corner system.
226 **Twister (12b)** ★★
227 **Dwarf Toss (12c)** ★★ Reachy.

Routes 228 through 237 are on what is collectively known as The Gridwall.

228 **Invitation to the Blues (11d)** ★★
229 **Small Change (11a)** ★ A decent warm-up route.
230 **Erection or Ejection (11d)** ★★
231 **Music for Chameleons (11d)** ★★ Great pockets.
232 **Death of a Sailsman (12a)** ★★ A plumb line up the center of the wall.
233 **Gridlock (12a or 12b/c)** ★★ Climb a tree to reach the first bolt and then step across, or climb the direct start (5.12b/c)You can traverse left to Death of a Sailsman's anchors to get off with one 50m rope.
234 **American Flyers (12a or 12b/c)** ★★ Many climbers have gained some frequent flyer miles on this jaunt. Climb a tree to reach the first bolt and then step across, or climb the direct start (5.12b/c). Remember to take the right fork.
235 **To Hell On a Rocket (12b or 12c/d)** ★★ The cruxes seem to be just before clipping the bolts. Stick clip the second bolt and winch up the rope to reach the starting holds, or climb the direct start (5.12c/d).
236 **Beeline (12b)** ★★★ Pocket perfection.
237 **The Anarchist (11c/d)** ★

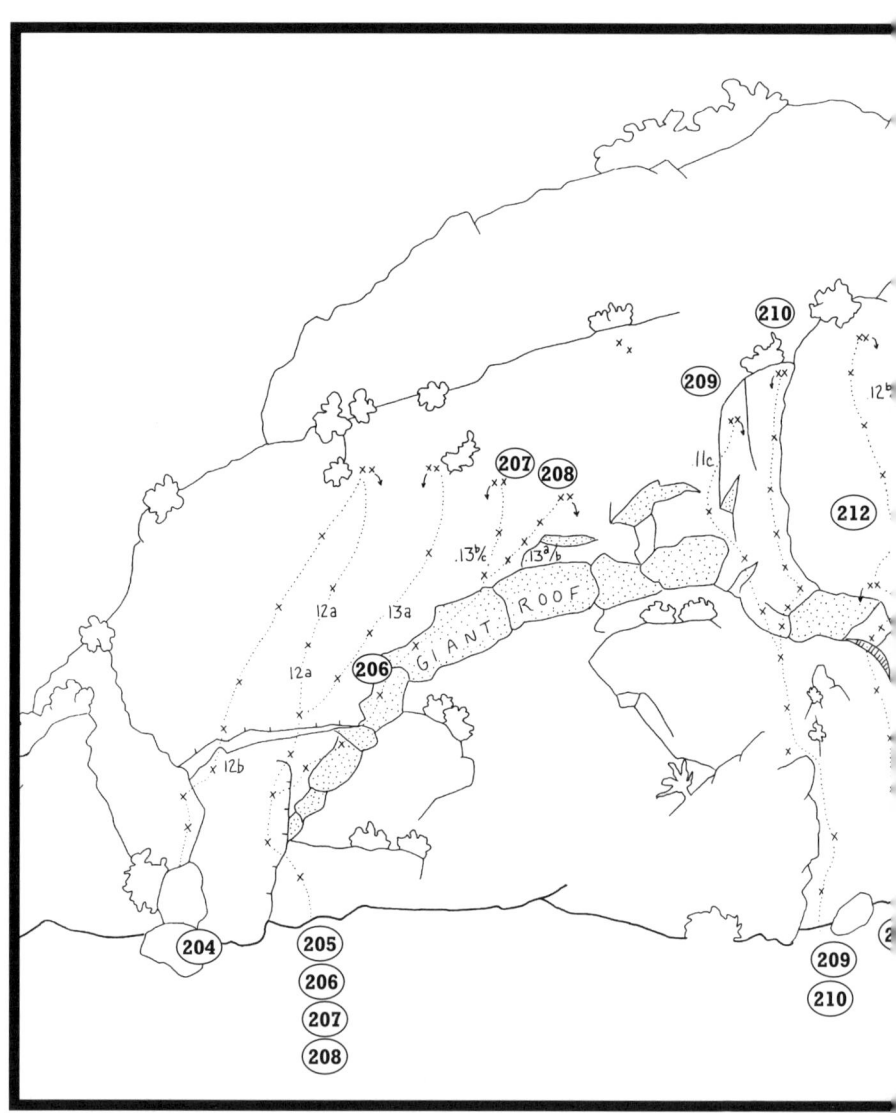

THE BILLBOARD

204 Gorillas in the Snow (12b) ★★
205 Appetizer (12) ★★★
206 Monkey Brains (13a) ★★★
207 Ghostdance (13b/c) ★★
208 The Final Sound (13a/b) ★★
209 Fang (11c)
210 Project
211 The One (12a) ★
212 The One That Got Away (12b/c) ★★
213 Eating the Gun (12d) ★★
214 Red Rum (13b) ★★★
215 Blue Murder (13c) ★★★

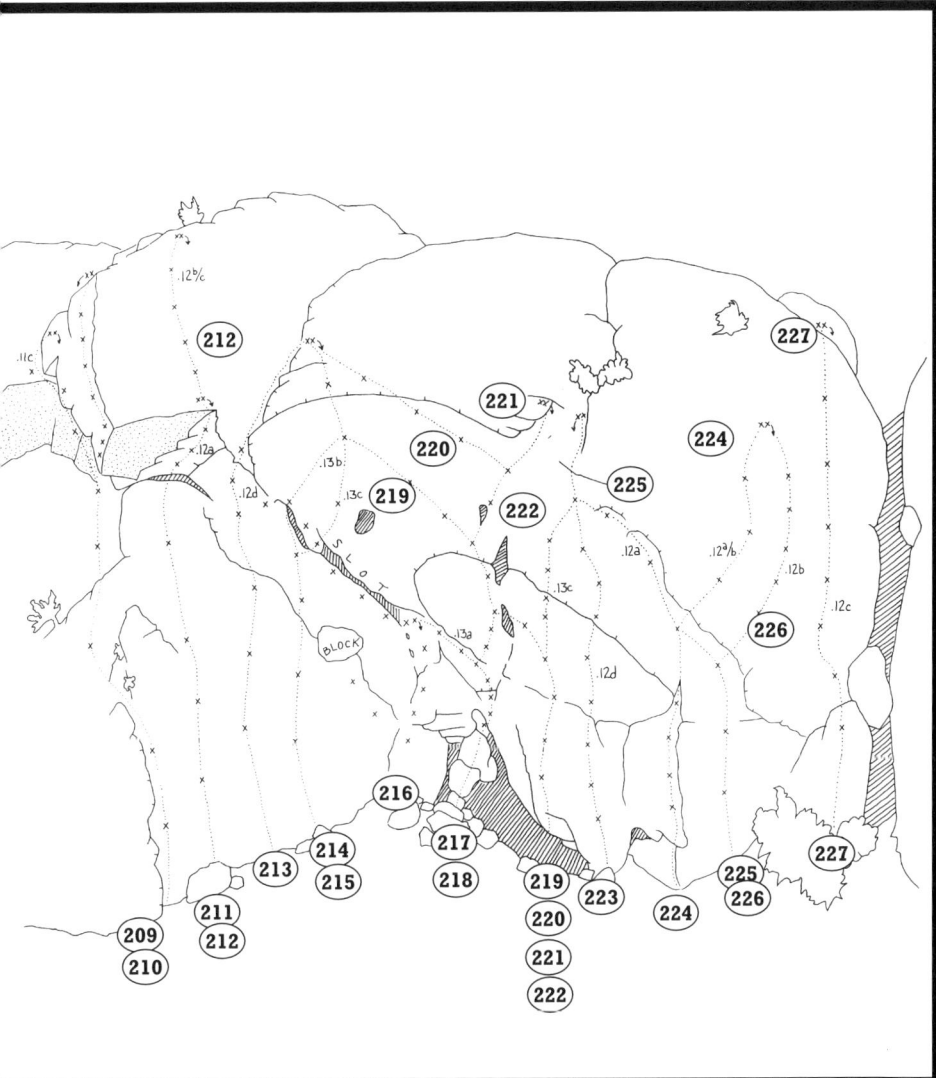

216 Project
217 Crack Baby (13a) ★★
218 The Hard Blues (14a) ★★★
219 Blue Mask (13c) ★★★
220 Invisible Man (13b/c) ★★★
221 Atmosphere (13a) ★★★
222 The Shining (13c) ★★★
223 This Must be the Pickle (12d/13a) ★★
224 Ambush (12a/b) ★★
225 The Whining (12a) ★
226 Twister (12b) ★★
227 Dwarf Toss (12c) ★★

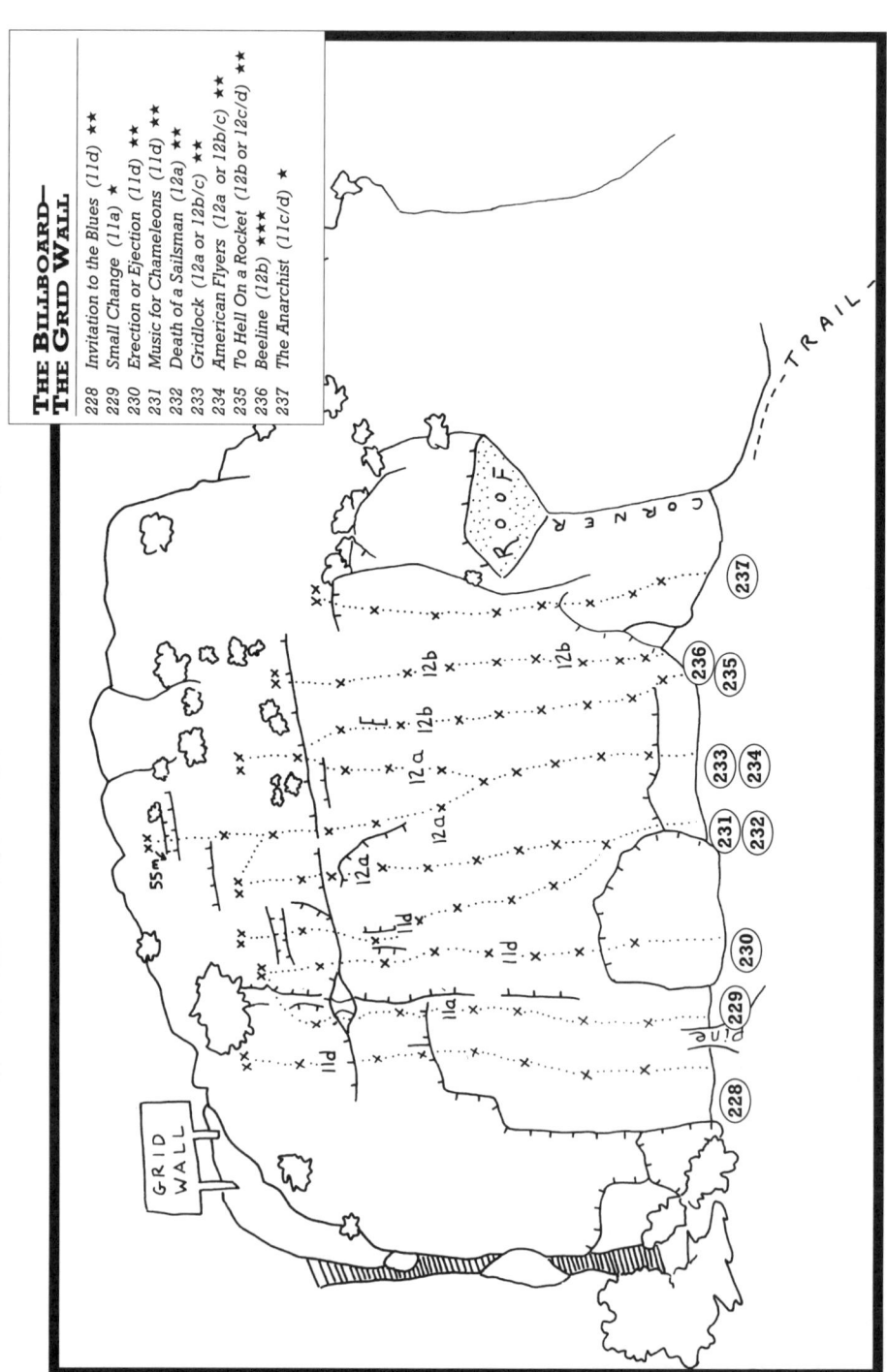

LITTLE MILL CAMPGROUND

The large campground 1.3 miles up from the Timpanogos Cave National Monument flagpole, has bundles of fine routes on some choice rock. The Division Wall is the single most popular crag in American Fork Canyon with a walloping 25 routes that climb through overhanging terrain on pockets and big edges. Quiet during the week, this campground transforms into a bustling hub of activity on holiday weekends. Wood smoke and the smell of frying bacon fill the air, and children run everywhere, wildly.

APPROACH Park 2.3 miles up canyon from the TCNM flagpole at several small pullouts on the right (south) side of the road. This is the exit to the Little Mill Campground, and a tire shredder prevents motorized entry from this direction. Simply walk back through the campground until campsite 64 is reached. The order listed below flows from east to west; the first cliff you'll see as you walk down the Little Mill Campground road is the Division Wall. Car-to-climb time: five to ten minutes.

DIVISION WALL

This wall is located just behind Campsite 64. Pocketed and steep, it is hard to go wrong with any of the climbs here. It can become crowded on summer weekends, however.

APPROACH See the approach information at the beginning of the Little Mill Campground section. Approach the Division Wall on the trail by the outhouse – don't cross through Campsite 64!

DESCENT It is possible to lower off chains at the top of each route with a single rope except for Secret Weapon and Isotoner Moaner. These two routes require a sixty meter rope. However, it is possible to lower off Isotoner Moaner with a single rope if you use the optional belay ledge.

- 238 **Liquid Oxygen (12a)** ★★★ A pumper finish that leaves most climbers breathless.
- 239 **The Abyss (12c/d)** ★★★ The most popular "project" route in the canyon.
- 240 **Shallow Beginning (11b)** ★★ A good combo of strenuous and technical.
- 241 **Deep End (11a)** ★ Steeper than you think.
- 242 **Black Hole (10a)** ★ Reachy and fashionably technical.
- 243 **Physical Therapy (9+)** ★★ A fingery route with an exciting arête.
- 244 **Teenagers in Heat (10)** ★ Mega pockets give way to edges.
- 245 **Litmus Test (11c)** ★★ The roof moves could change your color.
- 246 **Project**

Little Mill Campground • American Fork Canyon

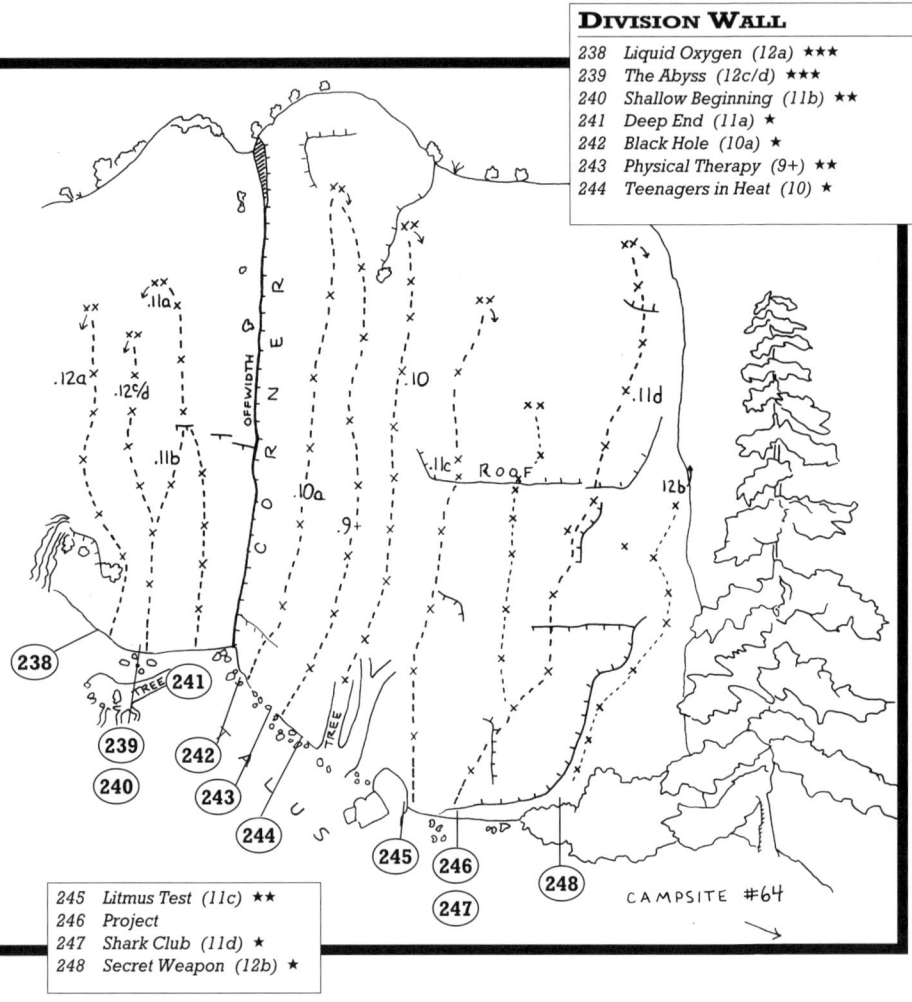

DIVISION WALL
238 Liquid Oxygen (12a) ★★★
239 The Abyss (12c/d) ★★★
240 Shallow Beginning (11b) ★★
241 Deep End (11a) ★
242 Black Hole (10a) ★
243 Physical Therapy (9+) ★★
244 Teenagers in Heat (10) ★

245 Litmus Test (11c) ★★
246 Project
247 Shark Club (11d) ★
248 Secret Weapon (12b) ★

247 **Shark Club (11d)** ★   Recreational climbing to a distinct crux.

248 **Secret Weapon (12b)** ★   Long, with a great upper face.

249 **Isotoner Moaner (12a/b)** ★★★   Long, with several distinct and varied sections.

250 **Rush Hour (11b)** ★★   Evenly spaced pocket pulling with a reachy crux.

251 **Remote Control (11a)** ★★   Slight runout to chains.

252 **The Atheist (11b)** ★★   Thin holds up top.

253 **39 (11b)** ★★   Continuously fun climbing.

254 **Running Woman (11a)** ★★   Don't blow the third clip.

American Fork Canyon • Little Mill Campground

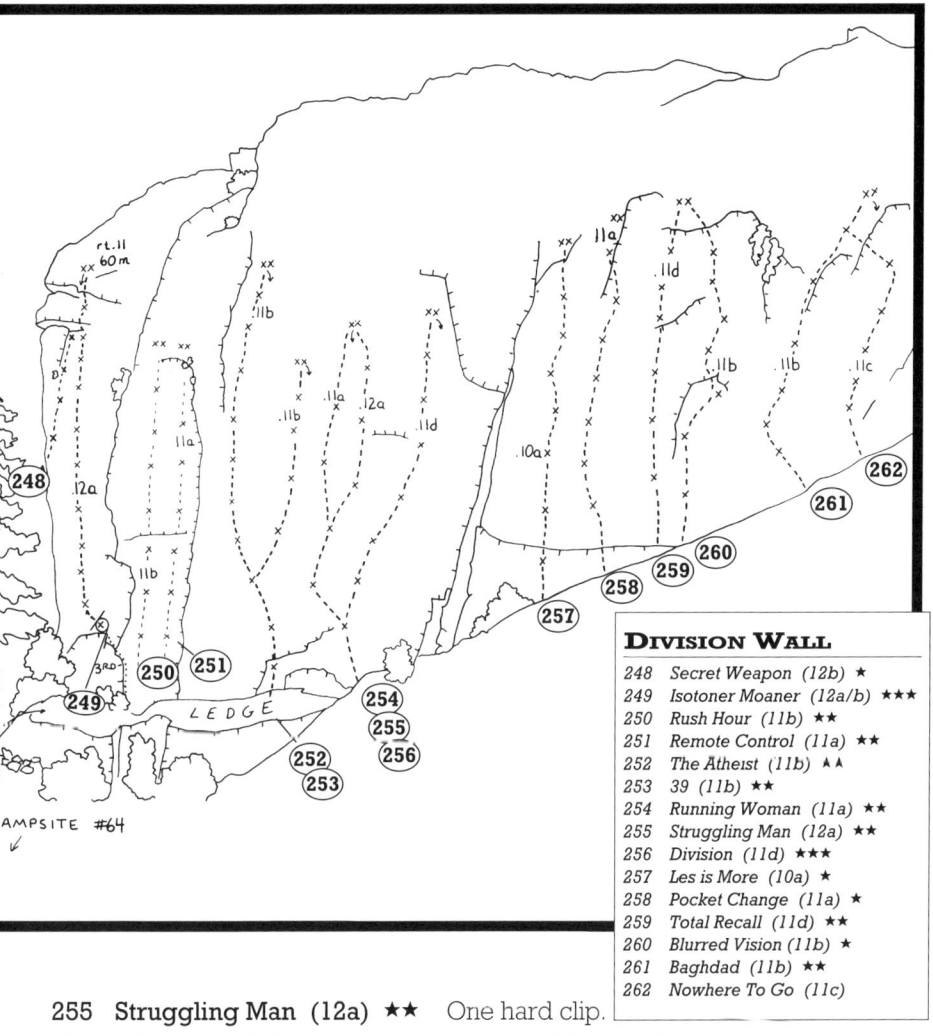

DIVISION WALL

248 Secret Weapon (12b) ★
249 Isotoner Moaner (12a/b) ★★★
250 Rush Hour (11b) ★★
251 Remote Control (11a) ★★
252 The Atheist (11b) ★★
253 39 (11b) ★★
254 Running Woman (11a) ★★
255 Struggling Man (12a) ★★
256 Division (11d) ★★★
257 Les is More (10a) ★
258 Pocket Change (11a) ★
259 Total Recall (11d) ★★
260 Blurred Vision (11b) ★
261 Baghdad (11b) ★★
262 Nowhere To Go (11c)

255 **Struggling Man (12a)** ★★ One hard clip.
256 **Division (11d)** ★★★ An archetypal AF route. Quality.
257 **Les is More (10a)** ★
258 **Pocket Change (11a)** ★ Save some spare change for the final moves.
259 **Total Recall (11d)** ★★ Tricky side pulls.
260 **Blurred Vision (11b)** ★ Some unique "handlebar" holds.
261 **Baghdad (11b)** ★★ Continuous, with long reaches.
262 **Nowhere To Go (11c)**

RATED ROUTE INDEX

5.5

| ☐ Layback Crack ★★ | 14 | ☐ Storm Mountain Stupor ★ | 14 |
| ☐ Nice Little Crack ★ | 14 | ☐ The Flake ★ | 18 |

5.6

☐ East Dihedrals ★★	14	☐ Six Appeal ★★	18
☐ Jig's Up ★★	14	☐ Steort's Ridge ★★★	14
☐ Schoolroom ★★★	47	☐ Tres Facile ★	22

5.7

☐ Beckey's Wall ★★★	48	☐ Schoolroom Direct ★★	47
☐ Bush Doctor	27	☐ Schoolroom West ★★	47
☐ Crescent Crack ★★	35	☐ Sweet Jane Variation ★	50
☐ Hatchet Crack ★★	47	☐ The Hook Variation ★	47
☐ Indecent Exposure Var. ★★	37	☐ Tingey's Terror ★★	50
☐ Perhaps ★★	42		

5.8

☐ Bushwhack Crack ★★	47	☐ Intelligent Life Form ★	25
☐ Callitwhatyouplease ★★	47	☐ Old Route	21
☐ Cranial Prophylactic ★★	42	☐ Pentapitch ★★★	50
☐ Fingertrip Variation ★★	48	☐ Satan's Corner ★★★	48
☐ Hand Jive ★★	35	☐ The Hook ★★	47

5.9

☐ Alpenbock Route ★	21	☐ Half-a-Finger ★★★	48
☐ Bad Faith ★	62	☐ Hollow Excuses ★	27
☐ Choir Boy ★	23	☐ Le Creme de Shorts ★★	14
☐ Chorus Line ★	23	☐ Lisa's Shoulder ★★★	48
☐ Crack in the Woods ★★	35	☐ Physical Therapy ★★	69
☐ Date With Fate ★	48	☐ Red Light District ★	21
☐ Gordon's Hangover ★★★	42	☐ (I9) S-Direct ★★★	37

Rated Route Index

5.9 continued

☐ Sasquatch ★★★	50
☐ Smitty's Wet Dream ★★	42
☐ The Coffin ★★★	35
☐ The Green Adjective ★★★	42
☐ Three Amigos ★	62
☐ Touch Up ★★	42
☐ Unknown ★	48
☐ Wheels on Fire ★★	45

5.10a

☐ Angle of Repose ★	25
☐ Black Hole ★	69
☐ Caress of Steel ★★★	62
☐ Gomer Pile ★	20
☐ Kermit's Wad ★★	42
☐ Les is More ★	71
☐ MA #1 ★★	42
☐ Mexican Crack ★★★	35
☐ Plumb Line ★★	37
☐ Private Hell ★	25
☐ Psychostematic ★★	20
☐ Tarzan ★★	50
☐ The Viewing ★★★	35

5.10b

☐ Cannabis Crack ★	62
☐ Dog Pile ★	20
☐ Endless Torment ★★	50
☐ Equipment Overhang ★★★	48
☐ Melting Point ★	21
☐ Morons of the Militia ★	27

5.10c

☐ Black and White John and Mary ★★★	48
☐ Blockbuster ★	25
☐ Cat Juggling ★	27
☐ Catalyst ★★	45
☐ Goodro's Wall ★★★	18
☐ Knobs to Gumbyland ★★	47
☐ Miller Time ★★	27
☐ Paranoia Streak ★★★	42
☐ Pencilneck ★	25
☐ Psychobabble ★★★	18
☐ Teenagers in Heat ★	69
☐ Tie Die ★	25
☐ Yuppie Love ★	27

5.10d

☐ Bourbon Street ★	23
☐ City Slave ★	22
☐ Clastic Cling ★	21
☐ Madison Avenue ★★	22
☐ Mind Blow ★★	47
☐ Old Reliable ★★	45
☐ Personal Jesus ★	25
☐ Rock Capades ★★	20
☐ Steel Monkey ★★	62
☐ Stem the Tide ★★	48

5.11a

☐ Black Monday ★★★	22	
☐ Dangling Participle ★★	42	
☐ Deep End ★	69	
☐ Earthling	27	
☐ Equipment Overhang ★★★	48	
☐ Eraserhead ★★	25	
☐ Eyes Without a Face ★★	20	
☐ Ionic Bonding ★★	21	
☐ Pocket Change ★	71	
☐ Remote Control ★★	70	
☐ Riptide ★★	62	
☐ Running Woman ★★	70	
☐ Small Change ★	65	
☐ Stick Figure Stays Home ★	27	
☐ Strong Arm With The Lads ★★	27	
☐ The Bungle ★★	47	
☐ Times Square ★	22	

5.11b

☐ 39 ★★	70	
☐ Against the Establishment ★	27	
☐ Baghdad ★★	71	
☐ Blurred Vision ★		
☐ Cheetah ★★	50	
☐ Gordon's Direct ★★	42	
☐ Lead Balloon ★	27	
☐ Looney Tunes ★★	45	
☐ Milling About ★★	25	
☐ Romeo's Bleeding ★	55	
☐ Rush Hour ★★	70	
☐ Sesame Street ★★	60	
☐ Shallow Beginning ★★	69	
☐ Skid Row ★	23	
☐ Stone Ground ★★★	27	
☐ The Atheist ★★	70	
☐ The Eye of the Enemy var ★★	18	
☐ The Odd Get Even ★★	27	

5.11c

☐ Cross Town ★★	23	
☐ Fang	64	
☐ Flashdance ★★	50	
☐ Gas Chamber ★	22	
☐ License to Thrill ★★★	62	
☐ Litmus Test ★★	69	
☐ Mass Wasting ★★	21	
☐ Mother of Pearl ★★★	45	
☐ Nowhere To Go	71	
☐ Rebel Yell ★★	20	
☐ S-Curve Overhang ★★	20	

5.11d

☐ Division ★★★	71	
☐ Erection or Ejection ★★	65	
☐ Exsqueeze Me ★★	35	
☐ Invitation to the Blues ★★	65	
☐ Little Big Wall ★	62	
☐ Moonwalk ★★	27	
☐ Music for Chameleons ★★	65	
☐ Reaching For Razors ★★	57	
☐ Right Pile ★★	20	
☐ Shark Club ★	70	
☐ The Anarchist ★	65	
☐ This Ain't No Party, This Ain't No Disco ★★	12	
☐ Total Recall ★★	71	

Rated Route Index

5.12a

☐ (12) Appetizer ★★★	64	
☐ (12a) All Chalk and No Action ★★★	42	
☐ (12a) American Flyers ★★	65	
☐ (12a) Badlands ★★	45	
☐ (12a) Death of a Sailsman ★★	65	
☐ (12a) Field of Screams ★★	62	
☐ (12a) Gateway ★★	60	
☐ (12a) Gridlock ★★	65	
☐ (12a) Half Acre ★	60	
☐ (12a) Jitterbug Boy ★★	57	
☐ (12a) Liquid Oxygen ★★★	69	
☐ (12a) Mandela ★★	62	
☐ (12a) Mission Control ★	62	
☐ (12a) Padded Cell ★★	18	
☐ (12a) Pile Surgery ★	20	
☐ (12a) Route 66 ★★	62	
☐ (12a) S-Crack ★★	37	
☐ (12a) Struggling Man ★★	71	
☐ (12a) The Blight ★	55	
☐ (12a) The Coffin Roof ★★★	35	
☐ (12a) The Enemy Within ★★★	18	
☐ (12a) The Maize ★	27	
☐ (12a) The One ★	64	
☐ (12a) The Whining ★	65	
☐ (12a) Trinity Right ★★★	45	
☐ (12a) Wasatch Reality ★	57	

5.12b

☐ Ambush ★★	65
☐ Beeline ★★★	65
☐ Big in Japan ★★	18
☐ Calling all Karmas ★	25
☐ Eye In The Sky ★★★	18
☐ Gorillas in the Snow ★★	64
☐ Isotoner Moaner ★★★	70
☐ Left Pile ★★	20
☐ Merciless Onslaught ★★	62
☐ Secret Weapon ★	70
☐ To Hell On a Rocket ★★	65
☐ Twister ★★	65

5.12c

☐ American Flyers ★★	65
☐ Dwarf Toss ★★	65
☐ Flight Fright ★	62
☐ Gridlock ★★	65
☐ High Life ★★★	21
☐ I'll Take Black ★	60
☐ Koyaanisqaatsi ★★	42
☐ Meat Puppets ★★★	42
☐ Nip and Tuck ★★	45
☐ Padded Cell ★★	18
☐ The Church of Skatin ★	55
☐ The One That Got Away ★★	64
☐ Think Tank ★	22

5.12d

☐ Amphitheater Overhang Left ★	18
☐ Bats out of Hell ★	57
☐ Eating the Gun ★★	64
☐ Guillotine ★★	55
☐ Reanimator ★★	57
☐ Something Wild ★★	62
☐ The Abyss ★★★	69
☐ Trinity Left ★★★	45

5.13a

- [ ] Atmosphere ★★★ — 65
- [ ] Crack Baby ★★ — 65
- [ ] Cross-Eyed and Painless ★★★ — 12
- [ ] El Diablo ★★ — 60
- [ ] Malvado ★★ — 60
- [ ] Melting ★★★ — 57
- [ ] Monkey Brains ★★★ — 64
- [ ] Oz ★ — 57
- [ ] Teardrop ★★ — 62
- [ ] This Must be the Pickle ★★ — 65
- [ ] Trinity Center ★★★ — 45
- [ ] Underdog ★★★ — 62

5.13b

- [ ] Burning ★★★ — 57
- [ ] Fallen Arches ★★★ — 45
- [ ] Hell ★★★ — 55
- [ ] Inferno ★★ — 60
- [ ] Jug Abuse ★★ — 62
- [ ] Red Rum ★★★ — 64
- [ ] The Final Sound ★★ — 64
- [ ] White Noise ★★ — 60
- [ ] Wizards ★★★ — 57

5.13c

- [ ] Blue Mask ★★★ — 65
- [ ] Blue Murder ★★★ — 65
- [ ] Fryeing ★★★ — 57
- [ ] Ghostdance ★★ — 64
- [ ] High Water ★★ — 55
- [ ] Invisible Man ★★★ — 65
- [ ] Linus ★★ — 57
- [ ] Side Show Bob's ★★ — 57
- [ ] Soul Fission ★★ — 60
- [ ] The Shining ★★★ — 65

5.13d

- [ ] Body Count ★★★ — 60
- [ ] Dog Eat Dog ★★★ — 20
- [ ] Power Junkie ★★★ — 57
- [ ] Satanism and Sports

5.14

- [ ] I Scream
- [ ] Cannibals ★★★ — 57
- [ ] Cop Killer ★★ — 60
- [ ] Dead Souls ★★★ — 60
- [ ] The Hard Blues ★★★ — 65